GCSE Spanish
VOCABULARY

Michael Buckby • Ken Hall

Heinemann Educational Publishers, Halley Court, Jordan Hill, Oxford OX2 8EJ
Part of Harcourt Educational

Heinemann is the registered trademark of
Harcourt Education Limited

First published in 1996

05
10 9 8 7

A catalogue record is available for this book from the British Library on request.

10-digit ISBN: 0 435378 58 9
13-digit ISBN: 978 0 435378 58 5

Produced by Goodfellow & Egan

Photographs were provided by Ken Hall

Printed and bound in Great Britain by CPI Bath

◀ *How to use this book* ▶

This book contains all the words and phrases you need to learn in order to do well in your Spanish exam. In some exams you may use a dictionary but if you know your key vocabulary you will be able to work faster and complete all questions in the time available.

The words and phrases are presented topic by topic. There are two sections – Foundation and Higher. If you are taking GCSE Higher tier you should learn both sections. If you are taking GCSE Foundation tier you should concentrate on the Foundation section.

Verbs are given in the infinitive form.

Adjectives are given in the masculine form only.

How to learn

Your learning will be much more effective and easy if you follow a few simple rules.

● Start several months before your exam: don't leave it to a last minute rush!

● Have regular and short learning sessions: 20 minutes three times each week is excellent, and better than one session of an hour.

● Before you begin a new topic, always go back and test yourself on the topics you have already learnt. This way, you won't forget them.

● When you learn, it is essential to use your brain actively. Do not just sit and read the words: do things with the words which will help you to understand and remember them. The activities below can be used with any list. Try several of them with each list until you have learnt all the words in it.

Activities to help you learn

Learning the words

● Try to learn eight to ten words. Then cover the English and look at the Spanish. Write the English equivalents and then compare what you have written with the book. Continue until you get them all right.

● Learn eight to ten words. Then cover the Spanish and look at the English. Write the Spanish equivalents and say the words to yourself as you write them. Then compare your list with the book. Continue until you get them all right.

● People tend to learn best the words at the start and finish of lists. To learn the words in the middle, re-write the lists and put the words in the middle at the top or bottom of your list.

● As you look at the list, write any words you are finding difficult to learn, omitting all the vowels (e.g. cuaderno – cdrno; rotulador – rtldr). Close your book and, looking only at your shorthand notes, write all the words in full.

- Make up a 'word-sun' as you look at a list. Write a key word in the middle and other words which relate to it at the end of each 'ray', e.g.:

al lado del mar

en avión

en verano

nadar

las vacaciones

quince días

pasar

al extranjero

jugar

Give yourself 30 seconds to 'photograph' this in your mind. Then cover up your 'word-sun' and try to write an exact copy of it. Compare it with the original.

Learning the sentences

- Try to learn six to eight sentences. Then write the first letter only of each word. Close your book and try to say, and then write, all the sentences in full. Check with the book and continue until you get them all right.

- As above, but writing just the first and last words of each sentence as your guide, plus the number of missing words. So, for '¿Qué quiere decir esta palabra?', you write ¿Qué ..... palabra? (3).

- Copy any sentences in the list which are true for you or your school or town, etc. Then change the other sentences so that they are true for you. So, for example, if you think that tennis is the best game in the world, you would write 'el tenis' in the place of 'el cricket' in this sentence:

  'En mi opinión, el mejor deporte del mundo es el cricket.'

- Use a ruler to cover up parts of some sentences when you think you know them. Then see if you can fill in the gaps. You can cover sentences in different ways:

No me gusta nada el marisco

Prefiero la ___ tatas fritas.

¿Le gusta el pollo asado?

- For any sentences which you find hard to learn, write the English on one side of a small card or piece of paper, and the Spanish on the other side. Keep these in a pocket or bag. Whenever you have a few minutes free, look at them in any order. If you see the English, say the Spanish to yourself and then look at the other side and check. If you look first at the Spanish, say the English to yourself and then check. Then shuffle the cards and do it again.

- You could make similar sets of cards, e.g.:
  - write a question on one side and the answer on the other;
  - draw a picture on one side to illustrate the Spanish sentence on the other side.

  Time yourself working on a set of cards and then try to improve on that time.

CONTENTS

FOUNDATION TIER

EVERYDAY ACTIVITIES

◀ *Language of the classroom* ▶

Classroom instructions

adivinar	to guess	**la atención**	attention
aprender	to learn	**una casete**	cassette
avisar	to warn; to inform	**una cinta**	tape
callarse	to be quiet	**una descripción**	description
colocar	to place; arrange	**un examen**	exam
contestar	to answer	**el fracaso**	failure
copiar	to copy	**la gramática**	grammar
corregir	to correct	**la hoja**	sheet of paper
describir	to describe	**la letra**	letter; handwriting
dibujar	to draw	**una línea**	line
diseñar	to draw	**un ordenador**	computer
entrar	to go in	**el papel**	paper
escribir	to write	**la pizarra**	blackboard
grabar	to record	**una presentación oral**	an oral presentation
hacer una encuesta	to carry out a survey		
leer	to read	**un problema**	problem
levantar la mano	to put your hand up	**el (la) profesor(a)**	teacher
levantarse	to get up	**una prueba**	test
mirar	to look at	**la respuesta**	answer
mostrar	to show	**el rotulador**	felt tip pen
obedecer	to obey	**el sacapuntas**	pencil sharpener
olvidar	to forget	**las tijeras**	scissors
opinar	to express an opinion	**la tiza**	chalk
parecer	to seem	**complicado**	complicated
pensar	to think	**demasiado**	too; too much
poner	to put	**difícil**	difficult
preguntar	to ask	**encima (de)**	above; on top of
proponer	to propose; to suggest	**exacto**	correct
		excelente	excellent
recortar	to cut out	**fácil**	easy
repasar los apuntes	to revise your notes	**fuerte**	strong; good
repetir	to repeat	**lentamente**	slowly
responder	to reply; to answer	**presente**	present
subrayar	to underline	**rápido**	quickly
tener	to have	**sobresaliente**	excellent
traducir	to translate	**por ejemplo**	for example
tutear	to address someone as 'tú'		

Intenta repetirlo con un buen acento.	Try to repeat it with a good accent.
Levantaos.	Stand up.
Ven aquí.	Come here.

Make classroom requests

ayudar	to help	un lápiz	pencil
cerrar	to close	un lápiz de color	crayon
dejar	to lend	una página	page
disculparse	to apologise	el permiso	permission
encontrar	to find	una regla	ruler
enseñar	to show	el servicio	toilet
explicar	to explain	una ventana	window
ir	to go	lo siento	I'm sorry
perder	to lose	perdone	excuse me
poder	to be able	por favor	please
prestar	to lend	a	to; at
un bolígrafo/ un boli	biro	¿cuál?	which?
una goma (de borrar)	rubber	otra vez	once more

¿Me dejas una goma?	Can you lend me a rubber?
Lo siento, pero he perdido mi regla.	I'm sorry, but I've lost my ruler.
¿Puede ayudarme?	Can you help me?
¿Puedo ir al servicio?	Can I go to the toilet?

Say if you (don't) understand

entender	to understand	sí	yes
no	no	un poco	a little

¿Entiendes?	Do you understand?
Sí, he entendido.	Yes, I've understood.
Lo siento, pero no he entendido esa frase.	I'm sorry, but I haven't understood that sentence.

Ask someone to repeat

decir	to say	una palabra	word
oír	to hear	en voz alta	aloud
querer	to want	menos	less
una frase	sentence	¿cómo?	pardon?; what?

¿Quiere repetir la pregunta?	Could you repeat the question?
¿Quieres hablar más despacio?	Could you speak more slowly?
¿Cómo? ¿Quiere hablar más fuerte?	Sorry, could you speak louder?

Ask someone to spell a word

deletrear	to spell	con	with
hay	there is	en	on

¿Hay un acento en la 'e'?	Is there an accent on the 'e'?
Se escribe con dos erres.	It's written with two 'r's.
¿Puedes deletrearme esa palabra?	Can you spell that word for me?

Here is the Spanish alphabet with a guide to how the letters are pronounced:

A	Like <u>a</u> in b<u>a</u>t.	K	Like <u>ka</u>.	T	Like <u>tay</u>.
B	Like <u>bay</u>.	L	Like <u>ellay</u>.	U	Like <u>oo</u> in b<u>oo</u>t.
C	Like <u>they</u>.	M	Like <u>emmay</u>.	V	Like <u>oovay</u>.
D	Like <u>day</u>.	N	Like <u>ennay</u>.	W	Like <u>doblay</u>
E	Like <u>ey</u>.	Ñ	Like <u>enyay</u>.		<u>oovay</u>.
F	Like <u>effay</u>.	O	Like <u>o</u> in p<u>o</u>t.	X	Like <u>aykis</u>.
G	Like <u>hay</u>.	P	Like <u>pay</u>.	Y	Like <u>ee griega</u>.
H	Like <u>atchay</u>.	Q	Like <u>coo</u>.	Z	Like <u>thayta</u>.
I	Like <u>ee</u>.	R	Like <u>eray</u>.		
J	Like <u>hotta</u>.	S	Like <u>essay</u>.		

Ask if someone speaks Spanish or English

inglés	English		**hablar**	to speak
español	Spanish			

¿Habla usted inglés?	Do you speak English?
Prefiero hablar español.	I prefer to speak Spanish.
No habla inglés.	S/he doesn't speak English.

Ask what things are called and what words mean

¿cómo?	how?; what?		**¿qué?**	what?
es	it is		**querer decir**	to mean
femenino	feminine		**significar**	to mean
masculino	masculine			

¿Qué quiere decir esta frase?	What does this sentence mean?
¿Cómo es en inglés/español?	What is it in English/Spanish?
¿Cómo se dice en español?	How do you say that in Spanish?

Say you do not know

saber	to know

¿Cómo se dice 'I don't know' en español?	How do you say 'I don't know' in Spanish?
No lo sé.	I don't know.

Say if something is correct

cierto	correct		**un error**	mistake
correcto	correct		**una falta**	error
falso	false		**estar bien/mal**	to be right/wrong
mentira	false		**tener razón**	to be right
verdad	true		**trabajar**	to work
una duda	doubt		**unos/unas**	some

¿Es correcto?	Is that correct?
No, hay una falta aquí.	No, there's a mistake here.
Hay algunos errores.	There are some mistakes.
Me he equivocado.	I've made a mistake.

Para mejorar la memoria

Improve your memory!
With some practice it's actually possible to improve and develop your memory! A French psychologist, Monique le Poncin, has invented a method for doing this. It involves exercising all your intellectual faculties – a bit like fitness training! According to Monique le Poncin, nearly all people who have problems with remembering things simply need to improve their powers of concentration. The fact is, it's actually impossible to forget something. You may have problems locating a piece of information but it's there somewhere! So improving your memory involves getting better at finding what you're looking for, and finding it more quickly.
Here's what you do:
- First, identify the information you want to memorise and concentrate on it.
- Then, associate the information with as many different things and ideas as possible.
- Use a variety of strategies to help you memorise – e.g. visual memory (pictures, lists, colours, etc.) and audio memory (record words onto a cassette).

Just as with physical training you need to exercise regularly. To get the most out of your training follow these tips:
- Work in a quiet room.
- Work in the morning or at the end of the afternoon.
- Make sure you get enough sleep – your memory will perform better.
- Don't try to memorise after physical exercise or after a big meal.

The *Para mejorar la memoria* activities like the one below will help you to train your memory. The important thing isn't getting the correct answer but doing the exercise!

Para mejorar la memoria 1

Actividad visual
Mira estos bolígrafos. Di, lo antes posible, cuántos bolígrafos hay.

Solución en la página 91.

◀ *School* ▶

Travel to and from school

en autobús	by bus	ir	to go
en autocar	by coach	ir a pie; ir andando	to go on foot; to walk
en bicicleta	by bicycle	llegar	to arrive
en casa	at home	parar	to stop
en coche	by car	salir	to leave
en metro	by underground	venir	to come
un colegio	school	volver	to return
una escuela	school	con retraso	late
una estación	(bus) station	cuando	when
(de autobuses)		normalmente	usually
un instituto	secondary school	porque	because
una parada de	bus stop	siempre	always
autobús		temprano; pronto	early
coger	to take	tarde	late

¿Cómo vas al colegio?	How do you go to school?
En invierno cojo el autobús.	In winter I catch the bus.
Esta mañana he venido a pie.	This morning I came on foot.
¿A qué hora sales de casa?	At what time do you leave home?
Normalmente salgo a las ocho.	I usually leave at eight o'clock.

When school begins and ends

un curso	subject	después (de las	after (lessons)
la mañana	morning	clases)	
el principio	beginning; start	durante	during
la tarde	afternoon; evening	media	half
empezar	to begin	menos	less
terminar	to finish	primero	first
a eso de	at about	segundo	second
antes	before	sobre	about
ausente	absent	tercero	third
cuarto	quarter	último	last

¿A qué hora empiezan las clases?	What time do the lessons begin?
La primera clase empieza a las nueve y cuarto.	The first lesson begins at 9.15.
Por la tarde las clases terminan a las tres y media.	In the afternoon, lessons end at 3.30.

Lessons: how many there are, how long they last

el alemán	German	una clase	class; lesson
una asignatura	subject	la cocina	cooking
la biología	biology	el corte y confección	needlework
las ciencias	sciences	un cuaderno	exercise book

los deportes	sports		la música	music
un día	day		un nivel	level
el dibujo	art; drawing		la química	chemistry
el drama	drama		la religión	religion
la educación física	physical education		la tecnología	technology
el español	Spanish		los trabajos manuales	craft
la ética	P.S.E.		coser	to sew
la física	physics		durar	to last
el francés	French		portarse bien/mal	to behave well/badly
la geografía	geography		practicar	to practise
la gimnasia	gymnastics		tener	to have
la historia	history		bastante	quite; enough
una hora	hour		¿cuánto/a?	how much?
un horario	timetable		¿cuántos/as?	how many?
el idioma	language		largo	long
la informática	information technology		normalmente	normally
el inglés	English		obligatorio	compulsory
una lección	lesson		práctico	practical
la lengua	language		cada	each
las matemáticas	mathematics		en mi opinión	in my opinion
un minuto	minute		por	pcr

¿Cuántas clases tienes?	How many lessons do you have?
Normalmente, tenemos cuatro o cinco clases por día.	Normally, we have four or five lessons per day.
¿Cuánto tiempo dura cada clase?	How long does each lesson last?
Normalmente, las clases duran cincuenta minutos.	Normally lessons last 50 minutes.
En mi opinión son demasiado largas.	In my opinion, they're too long.

Some important numbers:

diez	10		cuarenta	40		ochenta	80
quince	15		cincuenta	50		noventa	90
veinticinco	25		sesenta	60		cien	100
treinta	30		setenta	70			

Breaktimes and lunchtimes

un(a) amigo/a	friend		la hora de comer	lunch break
la amistad	friendship		mediodía	midday; lunchtime
la cantina	canteen		el patio (de recreo)	playground
un chiste	joke		el recreo	play time; break
la comida	lunch		charlar	to chat
un(a) compañero/a	colleague		comer	to eat
el fútbol	soccer		jugar	to play

¿A qué hora es la comida?	What time is lunch?
A las doce y diez.	At ten past 12.
¿Dónde comes?	Where do you eat?

Normalmente como en la cantina.	I normally eat in the canteen.		
¿Qué haces en el recreo de mediodía?	What do you do during the midday break?		
Charlo con mis compañeros.	I chat with my friends.		
¿Cuántos recreos hay?	How many breaks are there?		
Uno por la mañana y otro por la tarde.	One in the morning and another one in the afternoon.		

Homework

aburrirse	to get bored	un proyecto	plan; project
aprobar	to pass	aburrido	boring
comprender	to understand	difícil	difficult
darse cuenta de	to realise	estricto	strict
decidir	to decide	estupendo	great
detestar	to hate	fácil	easy
enfadarse	to get angry	inteligente	intelligent
equivocarse	to make a mistake	interesante	interesting
estar harto de	to be fed up with	inútil	useless
hacer	to do	torpe	slow; dim
inquietarse	to be worried	útil	useful
intentar	to try	acerca de	about
obtener	to get, obtain	a menudo	often
preocuparse	to worry	a veces	sometimes
sacar buenas/	to get good/bad	cada	each
malas notas	marks	en	in
suspender	to fail	mucho	a lot
los deberes	homework	mucho tiempo	a long time
un dormitorio	bedroom	muy	very
un montón	a lot	nunca	never

Tenemos demasiados deberes.	We have too much homework.
¿Cuántas horas de deberes haces cada noche?	How many hours of homework do you do each night?
Hago dos horas de deberes por día.	I do two hours of homework per day.

Extra-curricular activities

una actividad	an activity	el rugby	rugby
un campeonato	championship	una semana	week
un concierto	concert	una tarde	evening
una discoteca	disco	el teatro	theatre
una excursión	trip	el tenis	tennis
el fin de semana	weekend	una vez	once
un golpe	blow; hit	bailar	to dance
un grupo	group	encantarle a uno	to love
el hockey	hockey	escuchar	to listen to
un intercambio	exchange	gustarle a uno	to like
la música	music	nadar	to swim
la natación	swimming	odiar	to hate
un partido	match	ser socio/	to be a member of a
la piscina	swimming pool	miembro de un club	club
un polideportivo	sports centre	luego	then

¿Qué actividades hay en tu colegio?	What activities are there at your school?
Me encanta escuchar la música.	I love listening to music.
El fin de semana pasado jugué al hockey.	Last weekend I played hockey.
Soy socio del club de tenis.	I'm a member of the tennis club.
Ayer por la tarde fui a una discoteca.	Yesterday evening I went to a disco.

Days of the week:

domingo	Sunday		jueves	Thursday
lunes	Monday		viernes	Friday
martes	Tuesday		sábado	Saturday
miércoles	Wednesday			

Around the school

el aula (f.)	classroom		la oficina	office
el (la) alumno/a	pupil		el pasillo	corridor
la biblioteca	library		la sala de actos	main hall
el (la) director/a	headteacher		el uniforme	uniform
el gimnasio	gymnasium		adentro	inside
el laboratorio	laboratory			

Para mejorar la memoria 2

Actividad visual

Antes de hacer este ejercicio, repasa las páginas 1 a 8.
Mira estas bicicletas. Di lo más rápido posible cuántas bicicletas hay.

Solución en la página 91.

◀ *Home life* ▶

Jobs around the home

arreglar	to tidy	una aspiradora	vacuum cleaner
arreglar el jardín	to do the gardening	las cosas	things; belongings
ayudar	to help	un dormitorio	bedroom
barrer	to brush	las faenas de casa	the housework
comprar	to buy	el jardín	garden
fregar/lavar los platos	to do the washing-up	la madre	mother
		una mancha	spot; mark
hacer las camas	to make the beds	la mesa	table
hacer la compra	to do the shopping	el padre	father
ir de compras	to go shopping	los padres	parents
lavar	to wash	los quehaceres	household tasks
lavar la ropa	to do the washing	una tarea	job; chore
limpiar	to clean	un tornillo	screw
meter	to put	una vez	a time
necesitar	to need	a veces	sometimes
pasar la aspiradora	to hoover	de vez en cuando	from time to time
planchar	to iron	de vidrio	made of glass
poner la mesa	to lay the table	en	in
preparar la comida	to prepare the meals	entonces	then
quitar el polvo	to dust	generalmente	generally

¿Qué haces para ayudar en casa?	What do you do to help at home?
Paso la aspiradora.	I do the hoovering.
Ayer fregué los platos.	Yesterday I did the washing-up.
El fin de semana próximo voy a arreglar el jardín con mi padre.	Next weekend, I'm going to do the gardening with my father.

Your address and where you live

un apartamento	flat	una provincia	province
una avenida	avenue	una región	region
un barrio	part of town; district	el sur	south
una calle	street	una urbanización	urban development; housing estate
un camino	road		
una carretera	main road	la vecindad	neighbourhood
una casa (adosada)	(semi-detached) house	un(a) vecino/a	neighbour
		la vivienda	housing
el centro (de la ciudad)	centre (of town)	una zona	zone; area
		construir	to build
el código postal	post code	mudarse de casa	to move house
la costa	coast	vivir	to live
una dirección	address	enorme	enormous
el domicilio	home address	grande	big
el este	east	moderno	modern
un lugar	place	pequeño	small
el norte	north	tranquilo	quiet
un número	number	viejo	old
el oeste	west	en	in
un país	country	(estar) en casa	(to be) at home
una plaza	square		

¿Dónde vives?	Where do you live?
Vivo en ...	I live in ...
Está en el sur de Inglaterra.	It's in the south of England.
¿Vives en una casa?	Do you live in a house?
No, vivo en un apartamento pequeño.	No, I live in a small flat.
Mi dirección es cuarenta y cinco Calle Victoria.	My address is 45 Victoria Street.

Some countries:

Alemania	Germany		**Inglaterra**	England
Austria	Austria		**Irlanda**	Ireland
Bélgica	Belgium		**Irlanda del Norte**	Northern Ireland
(el) Canadá	Canada		**Italia**	Italy
Dinamarca	Denmark		**el Japón**	Japan
Escocia	Scotland		**Luxemburgo**	Luxembourg
España	Spain		**Noruega**	Norway
los Estados Unidos	the U.S.A.		**País de Gales**	Wales
Europa	Europe		**Portugal**	Portugal
Finlandia	Finland		**el Reino Unido**	the United Kingdom
Francia	France		**Suecia**	Sweden
Grecia	Greece		**Suiza**	Switzerland
Holanda	Holland			

Describe your home and its location

agradable	pleasant		**un chalet**	villa; detached house
ancho	wide		**un edificio**	building
antiguo	old		**una entrada**	entrance
atractivo	attractive		**una finca**	property; plantation
bonito	pretty		**un garaje**	garage
caro	expensive		**una granja**	farm
cómodo	comfortable		**el hierro**	iron
conveniente	convenient		**la madera**	wood
espeso	thick		**el mar**	sea
estrecho	narrow		**la montaña**	mountain
feo	ugly		**un propietario**	owner
hermoso	beautiful; lovely		**un pueblo**	small town
horrible	awful		**un ruido**	noise
inferior	lower		**la sierra**	mountain range
inmenso	immense; huge		**el tejado**	roof
nuevo	new		**una vista**	view
precioso	lovely		**compartir**	to share
profundo	deep		**atrás**	back; backwards
redondo	round		**casi**	nearly
típico	typical		**cerca (de)**	near (to)
las afueras	outskirts		**delante (de)**	in front (of)
un balcón	balcony		**detrás (de)**	behind
un bosque	wood		**lejos (de)**	far (from)
el campo	countryside		**realmente**	really

Háblame un poco de tu casa.	Tell me a little about your house.
Es bastante pequeña.	It's quite small.
Tenemos un garaje y un jardín.	We have a garage and a garden.
Estamos cerca del centro de la ciudad.	We're near the town centre.
Es un barrio agradable y tranquilo.	It's a pleasant and quiet part of town.

Your home: the rooms, garage and garden; colour, size and contents

un abrelatas	tin opener	una puerta	door
una aguja	needle	una radio	radio
un alfiler	pin	el retrete	toilet
una alfombra	carpet; rug	un rincón	corner
una almohada	pillow; cushion	un sacacorchos	corkscrew
un aparato	machine	un salón	living room
un árbol	tree	una sartén	(frying) pan
un armario	wardrobe	los servicios	toilets
el aseo	toilet	una silla	chair
una bombilla	lightbulb	un sillón	easy chair
una butaca	armchair	un sofá	settee
una cacerola	saucepan	el suelo	floor
la calefacción (central)	(central) heating	el techo	roof
		un teléfono	telephone
una cama	bed	una televisión;	television
un casete	cassette; cassette recorder	un televisor	
		la terraza	terrace
un césped	lawn	un timbre	bell
la chimenea	chimney	un tocadiscos	record player
una cocina	kitchen	un tocador	dressing table
una cocina de gas/ eléctrica	gas/electric cooker	la ventana	window
		el vestíbulo	hall
un comedor	dining room	un vídeo	video recorder; video
un congelador	freezer	el wáter	toilet
un contestador automático	answer-phone		
		eléctrico	electric
una cortina	curtain	feo	ugly
un cuarto de baño	bathroom	grande	big
un despertador	alarm clock	pequeño	small
un dormitorio	bedroom	pintado (de)	painted
una escalera	stairs	varios/as	several
un espejo	mirror	debajo (de)	under
un estante	shelf	en frente (de)	opposite
un estéreo	stereo system	fuera	outside
una flor	flower	propio	own
el fregadero	sink	pertenecer a	to belong to
un frigorífico	fridge	remendar	to mend; to repair
un guardarropa	wardrobe		
una habitación	room	amarillo	yellow
el hogar	fireplace	azul	blue
una lámpara	lamp	blanco	white
un lavabo	washbasin	castaño	chestnut; brown
una lavadora	washing machine	claro	light
un lavaplatos	dishwasher	el color	colour
una manta	blanket	color naranja	orange
un microondas	microwave oven	gris	grey
la moqueta	fitted carpet	marrón	brown
los muebles	furniture	negro	black
una nevera	fridge	oscuro	dark
una pared	wall	rojo	red
el patio	patio; yard	rosado; color de rosa	pink
un piano	piano	verde	green
un póster	poster	violeta	mauve

¿Puedes describir tu casa?	Can you describe your house?
Tengo mi propio dormitorio.	I have my own bedroom.
Las paredes son blancas y azules.	The walls are white and blue.
Las cortinas son rojas.	The curtains are red.
Tiene calefacción central.	It has central heating.

Taking a bath or shower

el agua (f)	water		bañarse	to have a bath
un baño	bath		ducharse	to have a shower
un bidé	bidet		funcionar	to work
una ducha	shower		usar	to use
el grifo	tap		caliente	hot
el jabón	soap		frío	cold
una toalla	towel		tibio	lukewarm; tepid

¿Puedo ducharme, por favor?	Please may I have a shower?
Lo siento, pero de momento la ducha no funciona.	I'm sorry, but at the moment the shower isn't working.

Needing soap, toothpaste or a towel

un cepillo de dientes	toothbrush		olvidar	to forget
la pasta de dientes	toothpaste		(muchas) gracias	thank you (very much)
dejar	to lend		por favor	please
necesitar	to need			

¿Necesitas algo?	Do you need anything?
Sí, no me queda jabón.	Yes, I haven't got any soap left.
¿Puedes dejarme pasta de dientes, por favor?	Can you lend me some toothpaste, please?

Ask where rooms are

el aseo	toilet; washroom		al lado de	next to
una escalera	flight of stairs		arriba	upstairs
un piso	floor		por aquí	this way
la planta baja	ground floor		por allí	that way
el primer piso	first floor		¿dónde?	where?
abajo	downstairs		estar	to be

¿Dónde está el aseo?	Where is the washroom?
Está arriba, a la derecha.	It's upstairs, on the right.

Information about mealtimes

almorzar	to have lunch	**una comida**	meal
cenar	to have dinner	**la comida; el almuerzo**	lunch
comer	to have lunch; to eat		
desayunar	to have breakfast	**(tomar) el desayuno**	(to have) breakfast
merendar	to have an afternoon snack	**la hora**	the time
		la merienda	afternoon snack
la cena	dinner		

¿A qué hora comemos, por favor?	What time do we eat, please?
La cena es a las siete y media.	Dinner is at 7.30.
Desayunamos sobre las siete y cuarto.	We have breakfast at about 7.15.

Daily routines

acostarse	to go to bed	**quitarse la ropa**	to get undressed
afeitarse	to have a shave	**tumbarse**	to lie down; to stretch out
dormir(se)	to (go to) sleep		
peinarse	to comb one's hair	**vestirse**	to get dressed

◀ *Media* ▶

Understand information about TV programmes, radio, music and performers

un actor	actor	**una película cómica**	comedy
una actriz	actress		
un(a) autor/a	author	**una película de terror**	horror film
un(a) cantante	(male/female) singer		
un cartel	poster	**la prensa**	press
una comedia	comedy; play	**un programa**	programme
un concurso	competition; quiz	**el sonido**	sound
los deportes	sport	**un teatro**	theatre
los dibujos animados	cartoon	**la televisión**	television
		un tipo	sort; type
un documental	documentary	**empezar**	to begin
un drama	drama	**poner**	to show; to put on
un(a) escritor/a	writer	**terminar**	to end
una estrella	star	**trabajar**	to work
la música pop	pop music	**(ser) aburrido**	(to be) boring
un músico	musician	**clásico**	classical
las noticias	news	**divertido**	funny
una película romántica	love film	**enamorado**	in love
		famoso	famous
una película de aventuras	adventure film	**fantástico**	fantastic
		increíble	great
una película policíaca	detective film	**se trata de**	it's about
		sumamente	extremely

¿Qué hay en la televisión esta noche?	What's on TV tonight?
Hay una buena película cómica.	There's a good comedy film.
Hay un programa de música pop.	There's a pop music programme.
Empieza a las nueve.	It starts at 9 o'clock.

Ask permission to use the telephone, radio, TV

apagar	to switch off	llamar (por teléfono)	to telephone
encender	to switch on		
escuchar	to listen	telefonear	to telephone
ver	to watch	una llamada (telefónica)	phone call

¿Puedo llamar a mi madre, por favor?	May I telephone my mother, please?
¿Puedo ver la televisión esta noche, por favor?	May I watch TV tonight, please?
Sí, enciéndela si quieres.	Yes, switch it on, if you want.

Talking about films/programmes/plays seen recently

una canción	song	ayer	yesterday
un cine	cinema	ir a ver	to go and see
un concierto	concert	oír	to hear
una noche	night	durante	during
una semana	week	hace (tres días)	(3 days) ago
una tarde	evening	pasado	last
antes de ayer	the day before yesterday	último	latest

Vi una película muy buena el sábado pasado.	I saw a very good film last Saturday.
Antes de ayer, fui a oír un concierto de música clásica.	The day before yesterday I went to a classical music concert.
¿Ha visto usted la última película de Almodóvar?	Have you seen Almodóvar's latest film?

Opinions about newspapers, magazines, TV, music

asustar(se)	to frighten (to be frightened)	joven	young
		malo	bad
atreverse a	to dare to	maravilloso	wonderful
cantar	to sing	moderno	modern
estar bien	to be good	negativo	negative
leer	to read	sospechoso	suspicious
llorar	to cry	un juego de vídeo	video game
pensar	to think	una lágrima	tear
preferir	to prefer	una obra de teatro	play
reír	to laugh	una opinión	opinion
silbar	to whistle	un periódico	newspaper
sonreír	to smile	una revista	magazine
sorprender	to surprise	un riesgo	risk
bueno	good	una risa	laugh
emocionante	exciting	un susto	fright, scare
extraordinario	extraordinary	un tebeo	comic
feo	ugly; lousy	muy bien	great
gracioso	funny	pero	but
interesante	interesting	todo el mundo	everyone

Sí, es muy gracioso, ¿no?	Yes, it's very funny, isn't it?
Yo no leo el periódico porque es aburrido.	I don't read the paper because it's boring.
Me gusta mucho ver la tele.	I really like watching TV.
Esta revista es emocionante.	This magazine is exciting.
El concierto de anoche no estuvo bien.	Last night's concert was no good.

Ask if someone agrees

estar de acuerdo	to agree		ella	she; it
ser	to be		sí	yes
conmigo	with me		también	also
contigo	with you		vale	O.K.
él	he; it			

¿Estás de acuerdo conmigo?	Do you agree?
Sí, estoy de acuerdo contigo.	I agree with you.
¿Qué piensas tú?	What do you think about it?

Note: For narrating a simple item of news see page 59.

Para mejorar la memoria 3

Actividad verbal
Antes de hacer este ejercicio, repasa las páginas 1 a 15.
En cada palabra/frase faltan dos letras. Escribe las palabras completas, lo más rápido posible.

1	una película p_licía_a	6	un ce_illo de di_ntes
2	el de_a_uno	7	un l_vapla_os
3	In_late_ra	8	una b_ta_a
4	el _eino Un_do	9	e_ocionan_e
5	el dor_itor_o	10	la na_ació_

Solución en la página 91.

◀ *Health and fitness* ▶

How you feel

encontrarse mejor	to be better		morir	to die
estar cansado	to be tired		bien	well; O.K.
estar enfermo	to be ill		fatal	awful
estar mal	to be unwell		herido	injured
estar resfriado	to have a cold		mareado	dizzy
sentirse	to feel		mejor	better
tener hambre	to be hungry		muerto	dead
tener miedo	to be afraid		quizás	perhaps
tener sed	to be thirsty		regular	so-so
tener sueño	to feel sleepy			

¿Cómo estás?	How are you?		
Bien, gracias.	Fine, thanks.		
Me encuentro mal.	I don't feel well.		
Me encuentro mejor.	I'm feeling better.		
Tengo calor/frío.	I'm hot/cold.		
¿Tienes hambre?	Are you hungry?		
Tenía mucha sed.	I was very thirsty.		

Say where you have a pain; explaining the problem

un accidente	accident	**un ojo**	eye
la boca	mouth	**una oreja**	ear
un brazo	arm	**el pelo**	hair
los cabellos	hair	**una picadura**	sting
la cabeza	head	**un pie**	foot
la cara	face	**una pierna**	leg
el codo	elbow	**una quemadura**	(sun)burn
el corazón	heart	**(de sol)**	
el cuello	neck	**una rodilla**	knee
el cuerpo	body	**el rostro**	face
un dedo	finger	**el vientre**	stomach
un diente	tooth	**caer(se)**	to fall (over)
la edad	age	**doler**	to hurt
una enfermedad	illness	**hacer(se) daño**	to hurt (oneself)
la espalda	back	**moverse**	to move
el estómago	stomach	**romper**	to break
la garganta	throat	**tener calor**	to be hot
la gripe	flu; influenza	**tener dolor de ...**	to have a pain in ...
una insolación	sunstroke	**tener frío**	to be cold
una mano	hand	**allí**	there
una muela	back tooth	**aquí**	here
la nariz	nose	**¡ay!**	ouch!

¿Dónde le duele?	Where does it hurt?
Tengo dolor de cabeza (muelas).	I've got a headache (toothache).
Me duele la espalda (el estómago).	My back (stomach) hurts.
Me caí.	I fell down.
Me he hecho daño en la pierna.	I hurt my leg.
Me duele aquí.	It hurts here.

Call for help

¡cuidado!	be careful!	**peligroso**	nasty; dangerous
¡ojo!	look out!	**¡socorro!**	help!

¡Socorro!	Help!
¿Puede ayudarme, por favor?	Can you help me, please?
¡Cuidado! El perro es peligroso.	Be careful! The dog's dangerous.

Note: For consulting a doctor, dentist or chemist see page 61.

◀ *Food* ▶

el agua mineral (f)	mineral water	un melón	melon
la alimentación	food	una naranja	orange
un albaricoque	apricot	un olor	smell
un aperitivo	aperitif	el pan	bread
el atún	tuna	el pan de molde	sliced loaf
una barra de pan	(unsliced) loaf	la pasta	pasta
el bistec	beefsteak	una patata	potato
un caramelo	sweet	las patatas fritas	chips; crisps
la carne	meat	el paté	pâté
los cereales	cereals	una pera	pear
una cereza	cherry	el pescado	fish
la cerveza	beer	la pizza	pizza
los champiñones	mushrooms	un plátano	banana
el chocolate	chocolate	un plato	dish; plate
una ciruela	plum	un pollo	chicken
una col	cabbage	un pomelo	grapefruit
el cordero	lamb	el queso	cheese
la crema	cream	una salchicha	sausage
la ensalada	salad; lettuce	el salchichón	salami sausage
los espaguetis	spaghetti	la salsa	sauce; gravy
el espárrago	asparagus	la ternera	veal; beef
las espinacas	spinach	un tomate	tomato
una frambuesa	raspberry	las tostadas	toast
una fresa	strawberry	una trucha	trout
la fruta	fruit	el turrón	nougat
una hamburguesa	hamburger	la uva	grape
un huevo	egg	las verduras	greens; vegetables
el jamón de york	boiled ham	una zanahoria	carrot
el jamón serrano	cured ham	beber	to drink
las judías verdes	French beans	comer	to eat
la leche	milk	asado	roasted
la lechuga	lettuce	fresco	fresh; cool
las legumbres	vegetables	vegetariano	vegetarian
una manzana	apple	con gas	fizzy
un melocotón	peach	sin gas	still

¿Le gusta el jamón?	Do you like ham?
No, soy vegetariano/a.	No, I'm a vegetarian.
Me encantan las legumbres.	I love vegetables.
No me gusta nada el pescado.	I hate fish.
Prefiero el queso.	I prefer cheese.
Las frambuesas son deliciosas.	Raspberries are delicious.

una almendra	almond	un pimiento	pepper
una cebolla	onion	una piña	pineapple
el chorizo	spicy sausage	la sopa	soup
una chuleta	chop	el té	tea
la coliflor	cauliflower	delicioso	delicious
los guisantes	peas	frito	fried
el pastel	cake	gustarle a uno	to like

invitar	to invite		bastante	enough
querer	to want		más	more

¿Quiere más coliflor?	Would you like some more cauliflower?
No, gracias, tengo bastante.	No thank you, I have enough.
Estaba delicioso. He comido muy bien.	It was delicious. I've eaten very well.
Gracias, pero no quiero beber más.	Thank you, but I don't want anything else to drink.

Ask for food and table items

el aceite	oil		la miel	honey
el azúcar	sugar		la mostaza	mustard
una cafetera	coffee-pot		el panecillo	bread roll
una copa	(wine) glass		la pimienta	pepper
un cuchillo	knife		un platillo	saucer
una cuchara	spoon		la sal	salt
una galleta	biscuit		una servilleta	napkin; serviette
una gaseosa	fizzy drink		una taza	cup
una jarra (de agua)	jug (of water)		un tenedor	fork
el mantel	tablecloth		un vaso	glass
la mantequilla	butter		el vinagre	vinegar
la mermelada	jam		pasar	to pass

Perdone, pero no tengo un vaso.	Excuse me, but I haven't got a glass.
¿Me pasa el pan, por favor?	Pass me the bread, please.
¿Tiene pimienta, por favor?	Do you have some pepper, please?
Este mantel está sucio.	This tablecloth is dirty.

A la prueba

How much does a cheese sandwich cost?

Call the waiter or waitress

un camarero	waiter
una camarera	waitress
¡oiga!	excuse me!
señor	sir
señora	madam
señorita	miss

¡Oiga señor/ señorita, por favor!	(To attract the waiter's/waitress's attention)

Solución en la página 91.

Order a drink or simple meal

una aceituna	olive	un refresco	soft drink
el arroz	rice	un restaurante	restaurant
una bandeja	tray	el sabor	flavour
un bar	bar	un sandwich	toasted sandwich
una bebida	drink	la sangría	sangría (drink made
un bocadillo	sandwich		with red wine,
una botella	bottle		lemonade and fresh
un café con leche	white coffee		fruit)
un café sólo	black coffee	una sardina	sardine
una cafetería	café	las tapas	snacks
la carta	menu	una tarta	tart; pie
la coca-cola	coca cola	una tortilla	omelette
un coñac	brandy	la vainilla	vanilla
el cordero	lamb	el vino (tinto/	(red/white/rosé) wine
los entremeses	starters	blanco/rosado)	
las gambas	prawns	un zumo de fruta	fruit juice
una hamburguesería	burger bar	comenzar	to begin, start
		picar	to pick at; to nibble
un jerez	sherry	tomar	to have (food and
un limón	lemon		drink)
la limonada	lemonade	traer	to bring
el marisco	seafood	dulce	sweet
una naranjada	orange drink	ligero	light
un perrito caliente	hot-dog	seco	dry
un plato combinado	set main course	variado	varied
una ración	portion	¡salud!	cheers!; good health!

¡Tráigame la carta, por favor!	Bring me the menu, please.
¿Ha elegido usted?	Have you chosen?
Para comenzar, la ensalada de marisco.	To start with, the seafood salad.
Después voy a tomar ternera con arroz.	Then I'll have veal with rice.
Y ¿para beber?	And to drink?
Un zumo de naranja, por favor.	An orange juice, please.

Ask about availability/Ask for a fixed price menu

los calamares	squid	el plato del día	dish of the day
un filete	steak	el plato principal	main course
un flan	creme caramel	un postre	dessert
los guisantes	peas	el primer plato	first course
un helado	ice cream	el yogur	yoghurt
la lista de vinos	wine list	empezar	to start
el menú del día	fixed price menu;	pedir	to order; to ask for
	tourist menu	adicional	extra; in addition
la paella	paella (rice dish with	incluido	included
	meat and/or		
	shellfish)		

¿Qué bocadillos tiene?	What sorts of sandwiches have you got?
¿Hay una lista de vinos?	Is there a wine list?
¿Qué desea?	What would you like?
Voy a pedir el menú del día.	I'm going to order the fixed price menu.
¡Que aproveche!	Bon appetit!

Ask for an explanation

el ajo	garlic		hervir	to boil
los churros	type of doughnut		recomendar	to recommend
una especialidad	speciality		utilizar	to use
una sugerencia	suggestion		como	like
un tipo de	a sort of		exactamente	exactly
freír	to fry		sin	without

¿Qué es el gazpacho exactamente?	What exactly is 'gazpacho'?
Es una sopa fría de tomates, ajo y pimientos verdes.	It's a cold soup with tomatoes, garlic and green peppers.
¿Es un plato caliente o frío?	Is it a hot or cold dish?

Opinions about a meal

la mesa	table		delicioso	delicious
la nata	cream		rico	delicious
el servicio	service		excepto por	except for
estar bueno/malo	to be good/bad		todo	all; everything
satisfacer	to satisfy			

Fue horrible.	It was awful.
El servicio fue excelente.	The service was excellent.
Las patatas fritas están frías.	The chips are cold.

Ask where the toilet or telephone is

a la derecha	on the right		junto	together
a la izquierda	on the left		por allí	that way
abajo	downstairs		por aquí	this way
al final	at the end		una cabina telefónica	phone booth
al lado de	next to		el pasillo	corridor
allá	over there		los servicios	toilets
arriba	upstairs		el sótano	basement
cerca (de)	near (to)		los teléfonos	telephones
¿dónde?	where?			

Por favor, ¿dónde está el teléfono?	Excuse me, where is the telephone?
En el sótano, al lado de los servicios.	In the basement, next to the toilets.
¿Dónde están los servicios, por favor?	Where are the toilets, please?

Ask for the bill

la cuenta	bill		¿cuánto?	how much?
un error	mistake		incluido	included
una propina	tip		pagar	to pay

Camarera, la cuenta, por favor.	Waitress, the bill, please.
¿No hay un error?	Isn't there a mistake?
¿El servicio está incluido?	Is the service included?

PERSONAL AND SOCIAL LIFE

◀ *Self, family and friends* ▶

Information about self, family, friends, pets

una abuela	grandmother	una niña	little girl
un abuelo	grandfather	un niño	little boy
los abuelos	grandparents	el novio/la novia	boyfriend/girlfriend
un(a) amigo/a	friend	el padre	father
un año	year	los padres	parents
un bebé	baby	papá	dad
una chica/un chico	girl/boy	un(a) primo/a	cousin
un(a) compañero/a	colleague	la sobrina	niece
el esposo/la esposa	husband/wife	el sobrino	nephew
una familia	family	una tía	aunt
una fecha	date	un tío	uncle
un gemelo	twin	único	only
una hermana	sister	una viuda	widow
un hermano	brother	un viudo	widower
una hija	daughter		
un hijo	son	un animal	animal; pet
un hombre	man	un caballo	horse
la madre	mother	un conejo	rabbit
mamá	mum	un gato	cat
un marido	husband	un hámster	hamster
el matrimonio	marriage	un pájaro	bird
un mes	month	un periquito	budgie
un muchacho	boy	un perro	dog
una mujer	woman; wife	un pez	fish
el nieto/la nieta	grandson/ granddaughter	un ratón	mouse

Háblame un poco de tu familia.	Tell me a little about your family.
¿Tienes hermanos?	Do you have any brothers or sisters?
Soy hijo/a único/a.	I'm an only child.
Tengo un perro que se llama Scooby.	I have a dog called Scooby.

Describing self, family and friends

alegre	happy	cariñoso	gentle; caring
alto	tall	ciego	blind
amable	friendly	contento	happy
ambicioso	ambitious	cortés	polite; courteous
anciano	old	corto	short
animado	lively	cruel	cruel
atrevido	daring; adventurous	débil	weak
bajo	short	delgado	thin
callado	quiet	deportista	sporty
calvo	bald	divertido	amusing; funny
capaz	capable	divorciado	divorced

elegante	elegant	**rico**	rich
embarazada	pregnant	**rizado**	curly
escocés	Scottish	**rubio**	blond
estúpido	stupid	**santo**	wonderful
feo	ugly		(lit. 'a saint')
formal	formal	**sensato**	sensible
fuerte	strong	**sensible**	sensitive
furioso	furious	**serio**	serious
galés	Welsh	**severo**	strict
generoso	generous	**simpático**	kind; good-natured
gordo	fat	**soltero**	single; unmarried
gracioso	amusing	**sordo**	deaf
grueso	fat	**tímido**	shy
guapo	attractive	**trabajador**	hardworking
hablador	talkative	**travieso**	naughty
honrado	honest; trustworthy	**tonto**	silly
horrible	horrible	**torpe**	slow; dim
impaciente	impatient	**triste**	sad
inglés	English	**valiente**	brave
inteligente	intelligent	**una barba**	beard
irlandés	Irish	**un bigote**	moustache
liso	straight (of hair)	**unas gafas**	glasses
listo	clever	**el humor**	mood; humour
loco	mad	**las lentillas**	contact lenses
moreno	dark (of skin/hair)	**el pelo**	hair
nervioso	nervous	**el peso**	weight
orgulloso	proud	**echar a uno de**	to miss someone
paciente	patient	**menos**	
pelirrojo	red-haired	**llamarse**	to be called
perezoso	lazy	**tener ... años**	to be ... years old
pobre	poor	**tener el pelo ...**	to have ... hair
popular	popular	**tener los ojos ...**	to have ... eyes
responsable	responsible		

Mi hermana es alta y rubia.	My sister is tall and blonde.
Tiene diecinueve años.	She's nineteen years old.

Say where you're from, spell your name, street and town

el apellido	surname	**el nombre**	first name
la calle	street	**el pueblo**	small town
la ciudad	large town; city	**ser de**	to be from

¿Cómo te llamas?	What's your name?
¿Cuál es tu dirección?	What's your address?
¿De dónde eres?	Where are you from?

◀ *Free time, holidays and special occasions* ▶

Hobbies and interests

la acción	action	**el ajedrez**	chess
un aficionado	fan	**un árbitro**	referee

el atletismo	athletics	un pasatiempo	pastime
el baloncesto	basketball	los patines	(roller) skates
el balonvolea	volleyball	(de rueda)	
una bicicleta	bicycle	una pelota	ball
el billar	billiards; snooker;	el piano	piano
	pool	el ping-pong	table tennis
un(a) campeón/	champion	el premio gordo	jackpot
-eona		los ratos libres	free time
un campo	pitch; field	un teclado	keyboard
una caña de pescar	fishing rod	el tenis	tennis
las cartas	cards	la vela	sailing
la caza	hunting	un videojuego	videogame
el ciclismo	cycling	el voleibol	volleyball
una colección	collection	caminar	to go walking
un(a) computador/a	computer	cantar	to sing
una costumbre	habit	cultivar	to grow; develop
los deportes de	winter sports	empatar	to draw; to tie
invierno		entrenarse	to train
un disco compacto;	compact disc	ganar	to win
un compact disc		gritar	to shout
una distracción	leisure activity	gustarle a uno	to like
un equipo de música	music system	jugar	to play (games)
la equitación	riding	montar a caballo	to ride a horse
un estadio	stadium	patinar	to skate
el footing	jogging	perder	to lose
el fútbol	football	pescar	to fish
un grupo	group	practicar	to do (a sport)
la guitarra	guitar	preferir	to prefer
un juego	game	saltar	to jump
un juguete	toy	tocar (un	to play (a musical
la lectura	reading	instrumento	instrument)
la lotería	lottery	musical)	
un miembro	member	vencer	to defeat, beat
un monopatín	skateboard	ver la televisión	to watch television
una moto	motorbike	visitar	to visit
una novela	novel	desde hace	since; for
el ocio	leisure	preferido	favourite

A mí me gusta mucho tocar la guitarra.	I very much like playing the guitar.
Mi deporte preferido es el balonvolea.	My favourite sport is volleyball.
Juego al tenis todos los sábados.	I play tennis every Saturday.

Express simple opinions and agree or disagree with them

aburrido	boring	mucho	a lot
agradable	nice	muy	very
atónito	amazed	porque	because
valer la pena	to be worthwhile	¿por qué?	why?
ambos	both	sin embargo	however
en contra	against	yo tampoco	me neither

¿Te ha gustado la película?	Did you like the film?
Sí, era muy interesante.	Yes, it was very interesting.
En mi opinión ha sido un buen partido.	In my opinion, it has been a good match.

Describe a recent holiday or leisure activity

la aduana	customs	un valle	valley
un albergue juvenil	youth hostel	una visita	visit
la arena	sand	el windsurf	windsurfing
una azafata	air hostess	bañarse	to go swimming
un bañador	swimming costume	encontrarse con	to meet
la costa	coast; seaside	esquiar	to ski
el esquí	skiing	gastar	to spend (money)
una estancia	stay	hacer autostop	to hitch hike
una excursión	trip; excursion	hacer camping	to go camping
el extranjero	abroad	ir de vacaciones	to go on holiday
el flamenco	flamenco	nadar	to swim
una foto	photograph	pasar	to spend (time)
unas gafas de sol	sunglasses	quedarse	to stay
un lago	lake	recordar	to remember
una máquina de fotos	camera	regresar	to return
		sacar fotos	to take photographs
el mar	sea	suceder	to happen
una montaña	mountain	tomar el sol	to sunbathe
una ola	wave	volver	to return
la orilla	shore; bank	a mediados de (abril)	in the middle of (April)
un pasaporte	passport	al lado del mar	at the seaside
una playa	beach	en avión	by plane
un recuerdo	souvenir	en invierno	in winter
una región	region	en Navidad	at Christmas
el sol	sun	en primavera	in spring
la sombra	shade	en otoño	in autumn
un sombrero	hat	en Semana Santa	at Easter (Holy week)
una sorpresa	surprise		
una toalla	towel		
el turismo	tourism	en tren	by train
un(a) turista	tourist	en verano	in summer
las vacaciones (de verano)	(summer) holidays	turístico	touristy
		quince días	fortnight

¿Ha pasado unas buenas vacaciones?	Did you have a good holiday?
Hemos estado quince días en Portugal.	We have been in Portugal for two weeks.
Fuimos de excursión varias veces.	We went on several trips.
En Semana Santa, nos quedamos en casa.	At Easter, we stayed at home.

Los meses	The months	julio, agosto	July, August
enero, febrero	January, February	septiembre, octubre	September, October
marzo, abril	March, April	noviembre,	November,
mayo, junio	May, June	diciembre	December

Preferences and alternatives for going out

el ambiente	atmosphere	una discoteca	discotheque
una bolera	bowling alley	un espectáculo	show
el circo	circus	los jardines públicos	park; public garden
un club (para jóvenes)	(youth) club	la juventud	youth; young people
		un museo (de arte)	(art) museum

un parque	park		descansar	to rest
un parque infantil	children's playground		encantarle a uno	to love (e.g. ... to do something)
un payaso	clown			
un polideportivo	sports centre		pasear	to stroll
un zoo	zoo		yo también	me too
dar un paseo; dar una vuelta	to go for a walk			

¿Por qué no vamos a la cafetería?	How about going to the café?
Prefiero ir a un concierto.	I prefer to go to a concert.
¿Prefieres ir al parque?	Do you prefer to go to the park?

Times and prices – buy tickets for leisure facilities

un adulto	adult		el precio	price
un baile	dance		un programa	programme
una corrida	bullfight		una sala de fiestas	night club
un descuento	reduction		una sesión	performance
un día de fiesta	public holiday		un teatro	theatre
una entrada	ticket		un torero	bullfighter
un folleto	brochure		un toro	bull
una oficina de turismo	tourist office		abrir	to open
			bailar	to dance
una orquesta	orchestra		cerrar	to close
un parque de atracciones	theme park; fun fair		comprar	to buy
			costar	to cost
un partido	match		empezar	to begin
una persona	person		pagar	to pay
una piscina	swimming pool		reservar	to book
una pista	track		caro	expensive
una pista de hielo	skating rink		prohibido	forbidden
una plaza	seat		reducido	reduced
una plaza de toros	bullring		hasta	until

¿A qué hora empieza el partido?	What time does the match start?
El concierto termina a medianoche.	The concert finishes at midnight.
Tres entradas para sala tres.	Three tickets for screen three.

Pocket money

ahorrar	to save money		una libra esterlina	one pound sterling
aumentar	to increase		una peseta	one peseta
dar	to give		un regalo	present
ganar	to earn		la ropa	clothes
una cantidad	amount		mil	one thousand
el dinero	(pocket) money		por mes	per month

¿Cuánto dinero recibes de tus padres para tus gastos?	How much (pocket) money do you get from your parents?
Me dan cuatro libras por semana.	They give me £4 per week.
Trabajo en una tienda para ganar algo de dinero.	I work in a shop to earn some money.

Para mejorar la memoria 4

Actividad verbal

Antes de hacer este ejercicio, repasa las páginas 21 a 25.
Lee bien estas palabras. Intenta buscar, lo más rápido posible, las cuatro palabras en las cuales hay las mismas tres letras consecutivas.

baloncesto	vacaciones
ordenador	guitarra
compañero	región
distracción	ciclismo
caballo	pueblo
aniversario	extranjero
educado	tienda
apellido	descuento
ocio	reducido
información	regalo
balonmano	ahorrar
pasatiempo	

Solución en la página 91.

◀ Personal relationships and social activities ▶

Greet people

buenos días	hello; good morning	**Feliz Navidad**	Happy Christmas
buenas noches	good night (can be used as a greeting)	**hola**	hi
buenas tardes	good afternoon; good evening	**mucho gusto**	it's a pleasure to meet you
de acuerdo	all right	**recuerdos**	regards
¡diga/dígame!	hello (on telephone)	**saludos**	best wishes
encantado/a	pleased to meet you	**vale**	O.K.
Feliz Año Nuevo	Happy New Year	**sentirlo**	to be sorry
Feliz cumpleaños	Happy birthday	**también**	too; also
		la verdad	truth

Muchas gracias.	Thanks very much.
Te presento a mi hermano, Carlos.	I'd like to introduce you to my brother, Carlos.
Y ésta es mi hermana, Ana.	And this is my sister, Ana.

Ask how people are

estar bien	to be well	**estar regular**	to be so-so
estar fatal	to be awful		

Buenos días. ¿Qué tal?	Hello, how are you?
¿Qué hay?	How's things?
¿Cómo está usted?	How are you?
Muy bien, gracias.	Very well, thanks.
¿Y usted?	And you?
¿Qué pasa?	What's the matter?

Exclamations

¡Buen viaje!	Have a good journey!
¡Felicidades!	Congratulations!
¡Feliz santo!	Have a happy Saint's day!
¡Mucha suerte!	Good luck!
¡Olé!	Bravo!
¡Qué asco!	How disgusting!
¡Qué bien!	Great!
¡Qué horror!	How awful!
¡Qué lástima!	What a shame!
¡Qué pena!	What a pity!
¡Qué va!	Get away!

Make informal introductions

un(a) (íntimo/a) amigo/a	(close) friend		**conocer**	to know
un(a) amigo/a por correspondencia	penfriend		**presentar**	to introduce
			mayor	elder
los miembros de la familia	members of the family		**menor**	younger

Éste es mi amigo por correspondencia español, Miguel.	This is my Spanish penfriend, Miguel.
Ya conoces a mi amiga, Cristina.	You already know my friend, Cristina.

Invite someone to come in and to sit down

entrar	to come in		**sentarse**	to sit down

¡Adelante!	Come in!

Welcome a visitor

un abrazo	embrace; hug		**adiós**	goodbye
un beso	kiss		**bienvenido**	welcome
alegrarse	to be glad		**hasta luego**	goodbye
despedirse	to say goodbye		**hasta mañana**	see you tomorrow
recibir	to receive		**pronto**	soon

Bienvenido a nuestra casa.	Welcome to our house.
Voy a enseñarte tu dormitorio.	I'll show you your room.

Thanks for hospitality

agradecer	to thank		**próximo**	next
volver	to return		**querido**	dear
la hospitalidad	hospitality		**atentamente**	yours faithfully
feliz (felices)	happy		**de nada**	not at all
posible	possible		**perdón**	sorry

Muchas gracias por su hospitalidad.	Thank you very much for your hospitality.
Ustedes han sido muy amables.	You've been very kind.
Lo he pasado muy bien.	I've had a really good time.

◀ *Arranging a meeting or activity* ▶

Suggestions for going out

aparecer	to appear		**venir**	to come
ir muy bien	to go very well		**una fiesta**	party
salir	to go out		**libre**	free
sugerir	suggest		**allí**	there
tener lugar	to take place		**no me importa**	I don't mind

¿Quieres venir a mi fiesta?	Do you want to come to my party?
¿Por qué no vamos a una discoteca?	Shall we go to a discotheque?
¿Estás libre mañana por la tarde?	Are you free tomorrow evening?

Inviting someone

esta mañana	this morning		**pasado mañana**	the day after
esta noche	tonight			tomorrow
esta tarde	this afternoon; this		**invitar**	to invite
	evening		**preguntar**	to ask
mañana	tomorrow		**una invitación**	invitation

Hay una fiesta en mi casa	There's a party at my house
el lunes que viene.	next Monday.
¿Quieres venir?	Do you want to come?

Accept or decline an invitation

aceptar	to accept		**tener que**	to have to
acompañar	to accompany; to go		**ahora**	now
	with		**hace falta**	it's necessary
decidir	to decide		**imposible**	impossible
declinar	to refuse		**mejor**	better
preferir	to prefer		**mientras**	whilst
poder	to be able to		**por supuesto**	of course
quedar	to arrange to meet		**una razón**	reason
sentirlo	to be sorry		**una reunión**	meeting
tener ganas de	to feel like; to be		**si**	if
	dying to		**sí**	yes

Gracias por tu invitación.	Thank you for your invitation.
Acepto con mucho gusto.	I accept with pleasure.
Desgraciadamente no puedo ir.	Unfortunately, I can't come.
Lo siento, pero tengo que quedarme en casa.	I'm sorry, but I have to stay at home.

Express pleasure

una idea	idea	**simpático**	nice
contento	·happy	**con mucho gusto**	with pleasure

¡Qué amable!	How kind!
¡Qué buena idea!	What a good idea!
Estoy muy contento/a.	I'm very happy.

Arrange a time and place to meet

citarse	to arrange to meet	**con retraso**	late
esperar	to wait (for)	**de acuerdo**	O.K.
reconocer	to recognise	**delante (de)**	in front of
verse	to see each other;	**detrás (de)**	behind
	to meet	**¿dónde?**	where?
una cita	date	**hasta mañana**	see you tomorrow
una parada	stop	**hasta pronto**	see you soon
a la derecha de	to the right of	**hasta el**	see you on Saturday
a la izquierda de	to the left of	**sábado (etc.)**	(etc.)
¿a qué hora?	(at) what time?	**tarde**	late

¿A qué hora nos vemos?	What time shall we meet?
A mediodía, ¿vale?	At midday, O.K.?
Te espero delante de la discoteca.	I'll wait for you in front of the disco.
De acuerdo.	Right.

◀ *Leisure and entertainment* ▶

Ask what is on at the cinema

un cine	cinema	**jugar**	to play
una película	film	**poner**	to show
un tipo	sort; type	**hoy**	today
estrenar	to show for the first time	**¿qué?**	what?

¿Qué ponen en el cine hoy?	What's on at the cinema today?
¿Hay unos dibujos animados?	Are there any cartoons?
¿Qué tipo de película es?	What sort of a film is it?

Find the cost of seats and buy tickets

un asiento	seat	**una plaza**	seat
una entrada	ticket	**una sala**	cinema screen
un(a) estudiante	student	**una sesión**	performance
una persona	person		

¿Cuánto es, por favor?	How much is it, please?
Dos entradas para la primera sesión en la sala 1, por favor.	Two seats for the first performance on screen 1, please.

Starting and finishing times

un espectáculo	show		**hacia**	towards
empezar	to start		**pronto**	early
terminar	to finish		**tarde**	late

¿A qué hora empieza el espectáculo?	What time does the show start?
Sobre las ocho y diez.	At about ten past eight.
¿A qué hora termina el concierto?	What time does the concert end?
Hacia medianoche.	At about midnight.

Opinions about events

aburrido	boring		**interesante**	interesting
bueno	good		**malo**	bad
divertido	amusing		**regular**	not bad; so-so
emocionante	exciting		**un cuento**	story
feo	nasty		**la voz**	voice

¿Qué te ha parecido la película?	How did you find the film?
¿Te ha gustado el concierto?	Did you like the concert?
¡Estuvo fenomenal!	It was great!
En mi opinión, era muy aburrido.	In my opinion, it was really boring.

Para mejorar la memoria 5

La memoria inmediata

Antes de hacer este ejercicio, repasa las páginas 21 a 30.
Estudia esta tabla. Luego, cierra el libro e intenta dibujar una tabla parecida, escribiendo el nombre de cada artículo en vez de dibujarlo.

Solución en la página 91.

THE WORLD AROUND US

◄ Home town, local environment and customs ►

Your home town and region

las afueras	outskirts	una oveja	sheep
el alcalde	mayor	el paisaje	countryside; landscape
la aldea	village		
un árbol	tree	un parque	park
un ayuntamiento	town hall	una piedra	stone
un barrio	neighbourhood	una plaza mayor	main square
el borde	edge	un puente	bridge
un bosque	wood	un puerto	port
una calle	street	una red	network
el campo	countryside	una región	region
un campo	field	un río	river
una capital	capital	un sendero	path
un castillo	castle	una vaca	cow
una catedral	cathedral	antiguo	old
un cerdo	pig	bonito	pretty
una ciudad	town; city	feo	ugly
la costa	coast	histórico	historic
una distracción	leisure activity	importante	important
una flor	flower	industrial	industrial
la forma	shape	moderno	modern
una granja	farm	montañoso	mountainous
un habitante	inhabitant	ruidoso	noisy
la hierba	grass	tranquilo	quiet
una iglesia	church	situado	situated
una industria	industry	cerca (de)	near (to)
una isla	island	entre	between
un lago	lake	lejos (de)	far (from)
un lugar	place	nada	nothing
un millón (de)	million	Edimburgo	Edinburgh
una montaña	mountain	Londres	London
un monumento	monument	el Mar del Norte	the North Sea
una oficina de turismo	tourist office		

¿Qué hay que ver?	What is there to see?
Hay un castillo antiguo.	There's an old castle.
Es una ciudad industrial en el oeste de Escocia.	It's an industrial town in the west of Scotland.
Es una región muy bonita.	It's a very pretty area.

Show a visitor around your town

acercarse	to approach	mirar	to look
enseñar	to show	una comisaría	police station

un edificio	building	un hospital	hospital
una estatua	statue	una muchedumbre	crowd
una exposición	show; exhibition	un museo de arte	art museum
un folleto	brochure	una pintura	painting
una fuente	fountain; spring	turístico	tourist (adj.)
la gente	people		

¿Quiere usted ir al centro?	Do you want to go into the town centre?
Aquí tiene el ayuntamiento.	Here's the Town Hall.
Baje esta calle y tuerza a la izquierda.	Go down this street and turn left.

Travelling into town

un autobús	bus	un taxi	taxi
una autopista	motorway	el tiempo	time
una carretera	main road	un viaje	trip; journey
un centro comercial	shopping centre	ir andando	to walk
una estación de autobuses	bus station	salir	to leave
		en bicicleta	by bicycle
la estación (de RENFE)	the (railway) station	en coche	by car
		en tren	by train
el metro	underground	céntrico	central

Para ir al centro, ¿hay que coger el metro?	To go into town, do we have to take the underground?
Hay una parada de autobús cerca de casa.	There's a bus stop near home.
¿Cada cuánto pasa el autobús?	How often is there a bus?
Cada veinte minutos.	Every 20 minutes.

Important festivals

el Año Nuevo	New Year	la Semana Santa	Holy Week
una boda	wedding	una tarjeta	card
un cumpleaños	birthday	una verbena	fair; open-air dance
el día de Navidad	Christmas Day	el Viernes Santo	Good Friday
el día de Reyes	Epiphany (6th January)	casarse	to marry
un día festivo	public holiday	dar	to give
una feria	fair	ocurrir	to happen
una fiesta	holiday; festival	tener lugar	to take place
la misa	mass	especial	special
el nacimiento	birth	religioso	religious
la Nochebuena	Christmas Eve	Dios	God
la Pascua	Easter	el primero de enero	the 1st of January
un regalo	present	el dos de mayo	the 2nd of May
la religión	religion	el siete de julio	the 7th of July
el sacerdote	priest	el veinticinco de diciembre	the 25th of December

¿Cuál es la fiesta más importante para ti?	Which is the most important festival for you?
Me encanta el día de Navidad.	I love Christmas Day.
Recibo bastantes regalos.	I receive quite a lot of presents.

Understand weather forecasts

agradable	pleasant	la mañana	morning
caliente	hot	el (Mar)	the Mediterranean
claro	clear	Mediterráneo	(Sea)
complicado	complicated	el medio ambiente	environment
cubierto	overcast	la noche	night
ecológico	ecological	una nube	cloud
frío	cold	el pronóstico	weather forecast
madrileño	from Madrid	la sierra	mountain range
máximo	maximum	la tarde	afternoon; evening
mínimo	minimum	la temperatura	temperature
nublado	cloudy	el tiempo	weather
raro	rare	contaminar	to pollute
variable	variable	estar nublado	to be cloudy
buen tiempo	good weather	estar templado	to be mild
el calor	heat	hacer buen/	to be good/bad
el cielo	sky	mal tiempo	weather
el clima	climate	hacer calor/frío	to be hot/cold
la contaminación	pollution	helar	to freeze
la escarcha	frost	antes	before
un grado	degree	después	after
el hielo	ice	durante	during
la lluvia	rain	mañana	tomorrow
la luna	moon	más tarde	later
la madrugada	early morning; dawn	mejor	better
mal tiempo	bad weather	rápidamente	quickly

¿Qué tiempo hará mañana?	What will the weather be like tomorrow?
Según el pronóstico, estará nublado.	According to the forecast, it will be cloudy.
Por la mañana hará buen tiempo.	In the morning, the weather will be fine.

Understand and describe weather conditions

haber niebla	to be foggy	la nieve	snow
hacer sol	to be sunny	un relámpago	(flash of) lightning
hacer viento	to be windy	una tormenta	storm
llover	to rain	el trueno	thunder
nevar	to snow	flojo	weak
soplar	to blow	mojado	wet
una gota	drop	al mismo tiempo	at the same time

¡Qué tiempo tan horrible!	What awful weather!
Hace viento.	It's windy.

◀ *Finding the way* ▶

Attracting the attention of a passer-by

perdone	excuse me	Señora	Madam
por favor	please	Señorita	Miss
Señor	Sir		

Perdone, señora.	(What you say to attract the attention of a woman.)		
Perdone, señorita.	(What you say to attract the attention of a girl.)		

How to get to a place

a la derecha	on the right	**seguir**	to follow
a la izquierda	on the left	**subir**	to go up
al final de	at the end of	**tomar**	to take
al lado (de)	next to	**torcer**	to turn
allá	down there	**una carretera**	main road
antes de	before	**la circulación**	traffic
a través de	across	**correos**	post office
aquí	here	**un cruce**	crossroads
delante de	in front of	**las direcciones**	directions
detrás de	behind	**la distancia**	distance
en el centro de	in the centre of	**un hospital**	hospital
enfrente de	opposite	**una isleta (de tráfico)**	roundabout
entre	between		
todo derecho	straight on	**un mapa**	map
todo recto	straight on	**la N10**	the N10 road
bajar	to go down	**un plano**	town plan
coger	to catch	**los semáforos**	traffic lights
cruzar	to cross	**hasta**	as far as
doblar la esquina	to go round the corner	**luego**	then
evitar	to avoid	**por último**	finally
pasar	to pass	**todas direcciones**	all directions

¿Hay un banco por aquí?	Is there a bank around here?
Siga todo recto y cruce el puente.	Go straight on and cross the bridge.
Hay que ir hasta el hospital, y allí torcer a la izquierda.	You have to go as far as the hospital, and turn left there.
¿Por dónde se va al castillo, por favor?	How do I get to the castle, please?
Tome la primera calle a la derecha.	Take the first street on the right.
Está justo después de la isleta de tráfico.	It's just after the roundabout.
El banco está enfrente del ayuntamiento.	The bank is opposite the town hall.

Nearby or far away?

cerca (de aquí)	near (here)	**estar a ... metros**	to be ... metres away
lejos (de aquí)	far (from here)	**estar a ... minutos**	to be ... minutes away
estar a ... kilómetros	to be ... kilometres away	**otro**	other

¿La estación de autobuses está lejos de aquí?	Is the bus station far from here?
No, está bastante cerca.	No, it's quite close.
No está lejos.	It's not far.
¿Hay otro hotel cerca de aquí?	Is there another hotel near here?
Hay uno a tres kilómetros.	There is one three kilometres away.
La autopista está a diez minutos de aquí.	The motorway is ten minutes from here.

Para mejorar la memoria 6

¿Qué tiempo hace?
Antes de hacer este ejercicio, repasa las páginas 31 a 34.
Estudia estos símbolos durante un minuto. Luego, tápalos con un papel y, en menos de un minuto,
intenta escribir en español el tiempo que corresponde a estas coordenadas:

A2   B3   C1   B1   A   B   C

	A	B	C
1	NUB./CLAR.	TORMENTA	VIENTO
2	DESPEJADO	CUBIERTO	HELADAS
3	NIEBLA	LLUVIA	NIEVE

Solución en la página 91.

◀ *Shopping* ▶

Finding shops and supermarkets

Spanish	English	Spanish	English
un anuncio	advertisement	una pescadería	fishmonger's
una carnicería	butcher's	un quiosco	newsagent's
un centro comercial	shopping centre	la sección	department (in a store)
un cliente	customer	un supermercado	supermarket
una confitería	sweet shop	una tabacalera	tobacconist's
una droguería	hardware shop	un(a) tendero/a	shopkeeper
un escaparate	shop window	una tienda	shop
un estanco	tobacconist's	una tienda de comestibles	food shop
una farmacia	chemist's	una tienda de discos	record shop
una frutería	fruit shop	una tienda de recuerdos	souvenir shop
los grandes almacenes	department store	una tienda de ultramarinos	grocer's
un hipermercado	hypermarket	una verdulería	greengrocer's
una librería	bookshop	una zapatería	shoe shop
un mercado	market	buscar	to look for
una panadería	baker's	hacer la compra	to do the shopping
una pastelería	cake shop	ir de compras	to go shopping
una peluquería	hairdresser's	cercano	near
una perfumería	perfume shop		

¿Dónde está la panadería?	Where is the baker's?
¿Hay un centro comercial aquí?	Is there a shopping centre here?
¿Dónde está el supermercado más cercano?	Where is the nearest supermarket?

Opening and closing times

abierto	open	**abrir(se)**	to open
cerrado	closed	**cerrar(se)**	to close

¿A qué hora se abre el banco?	What time does the bank open?
Las tiendas están abiertas hasta las dos.	The shops are open until two o'clock.
¿A qué hora cierran, por favor?	What time do you close, please?
Cerramos de dos a cuatro.	We're closed between 2.00 and 4.00.

Items of clothing/Souvenirs

un abrigo	coat	**un traje**	suit
un bañador	swimming costume	**un traje de baño**	swim suit
un bikini	bikini	**unos vaqueros**	pair of jeans
una blusa	blouse	**un vestido**	dress
un bolsillo	pocket	**unas zapatillas**	trainers
un bolso	handbag	**(de deporte)**	
una bota	boot	**unos zapatos**	shoes
un botón	button	**de algodón**	made of cotton
un calcetín	sock	**de cuero**	made of leather
una camisa	shirt	**de lana**	made of wool
una camiseta	vest; T-shirt	**de nilón**	made of nylon
un chandal	tracksuit		
una chaqueta	jacket	**un abanico**	fan
un cinturón	belt	**un anillo**	ring
una corbata	tie	**una bolsa**	bag
una falda	skirt	**una cartera**	wallet
un guante	glove	**unas castañuelas**	castanets
un impermeable	mac; raincoat	**la cerámica**	pottery
un jersey	jumper	**una cerilla**	match
un legging	leggings	**una cesta**	basket
unas medias	stockings; tights	**un cigarrillo**	cigarette
la moda	fashion	**un collar**	necklace
un pantalón	trousers	**un disco**	record
un pantalón corto	shorts	**una guitarra**	guitar
un pantalón vaquero	jeans	**la joyería**	jewellery
un panty	pair of tights	**un monedero**	purse
un pañuelo	handkerchief	**una muñeca**	doll
un par de	a pair of	**un pendiente**	earring
un paraguas	umbrella	**un porrón**	wine jug (with long
un pijama	pyjama		spout)
una rebeca	cardigan	**un puro**	cigar
la ropa	clothes	**un recuerdo**	souvenir
una sandalia	sandal	**un regalo**	present
un slip	underpants	**un reloj**	watch
un sombrero	hat	**de oro**	(made of) gold
un sujetador	bra	**de plata**	(made of) silver

Price

barato	cheap	el precio	price
caro	·expensive	un producto	product
gratis	free	las rebajas	sales
gratuito	free	un recibo	receipt
el cambio	change	el valor	value
un cheque	cheque	la venta	sale; selling
un descuento	discount	costar	to cost
el dinero	money	pagar	to pay
un impuesto	tax	valer	to be worth
una lista	list	vender	to sell
una oferta	offer	incluso	included
una peseta (pta)	peseta		

¿Qué desea?	What would you like?
Quisiera un par de calcetines.	I'd like a pair of socks.
Número cuarenta y cuatro.	Size 44.
¿Tiene este impermeable en rojo?	Have you got this mac in red?
¿Qué talla?	What size?
Mediana.	Medium.

Weight, volume, size, container

un bote	jar; can	el tamaño	size (of items)
una botella	bottle	un trapo	rag
una caja	box; tin	un trozo	a bit
una docena	dozen	un vaso	glass
un gramo	gram	corto	short
un kilo	kilo	estrecho	narrow
una lata	tin	grande	large
una libra	pound	largo	long
un litro	litre	mediano; medio	medium
una loncha	slice	mucho	a lot
el número	size (for shoes)	pequeño	small
el papel	paper	vacío	empty
un paquete	packet	¿cuánto/a?	how much?
un pedazo	piece	¿cuántos/as?	how many?
un poco	a little	estar bien	to be O.K.
una talla	size (for items of clothing)		

Quisiera un kilo de peras.	I'd like a kilo of pears.
Deme una botella de agua mineral también.	Give me a bottle of mineral water as well.
¿Puedo tener un trozo de ese queso?	Can I have a piece of that cheese?
¿Así?	Like this?
No, un poco más pequeño.	No, a little smaller.

Non-availability – answer 'Is that all?'

devolver	to return, give back	**eso es todo**	that's all
necesitar	to need	**nada más**	nothing else
quedar	to remain; to be left	**no**	no
ser	to be	**no hay**	there isn't (aren't) any
servir	to serve		
¿algo más?	anything else?	**un poco más**	a little more

No quedan cerillas.	There are no matches left.
¿Eso es todo?	Is that all?
Sí, es todo, gracias.	Yes, that's all, thank you.

Opinions about items

bonito	pretty; beautiful	**típico**	typical
de moda	fashionable	**viejo**	old
diferente	different	**costar**	to cost
distinto	different; distinct	**llevar**	to wear
económico	inexpensive	**quejarse**	to complain
moderno	modern	**la calidad**	quality
nuevo	new	**la tela**	cloth; material

¿Te gusta mi bañador?	Do you like my swimsuit?
Es muy bonito.	It's very pretty.
Tu chaqueta está muy de moda.	Your jacket is very fashionable.

A la prueba

¿Qué dice la clienta?

A) ¿A qué hora se abre el banco?
B) ¿Tiene este impermeable en rojo, por favor?
C) ¿Cuánto es en total, por favor?
D) ¿Algo más?

Solución en la página 91.

Buying something or not

deber	to owe		**recomendar**	to recommend
probarse	to try on		**tener que**	to have to
quedar	to take		**(no) gracias**	(no) thank you

De acuerdo, me lo quedo.	Fine, I'll take it.
Es demasiado caro.	It's too expensive.
¿Tiene algo más barato?	Do you have something cheaper?
¿Qué le debo?	What do I owe you?

◀ *Public services* ▶

Ask where a post office, tobacconist's or letter box is

un buzón	letter box		**una tabacalera**	tobacconist's
(una oficina de)	post office		**estar**	to be
correos			**cerca de aquí**	near here
un estanco	tobacconist's			

¿Dónde está correos?	Where is the post office?
¿Hay un buzón cerca de aquí?	Is there a letter box near here?
Está delante de correos.	It's in front of the post office.

Sending a letter or postcard home

a Escocia	to Scotland		**al Reino Unido**	to the U.K.
a Gales	to Wales		**una carta**	letter
a Gran Bretaña	to Great Britain		**una (tarjeta) postal**	postcard
a Inglaterra	to England		**entregar**	to deliver; hand over
a Irlanda	to Ireland		**mandar**	to send
a Irlanda del Norte	to Northern Ireland		**por avión**	airmail

Quisiera enviar una carta a Gran Bretaña.	I'd like to send a letter to Great Britain.
¿Cuánto cuesta enviar una postal al Reino Unido?	How much is it to send a postcard to the U.K.?

Ask for stamps

un duro	5 peseta piece		**dar**	to give
un sello	stamp		**querer**	to want

Quiero un sello de cincuenta pesetas, por favor.	I want a fifty peseta stamp, please.

Finding a telephone

agotar	to use up	**llamar a cobro**	to reverse the
colgar	to replace the	**revertido**	charges
	receiver	**una cabina**	phone box
descolgar el	to pick up the	**telefónica**	
teléfono	receiver	**un teléfono**	public telephone
		público	

¿Hay un teléfono público cerca de aquí?   Is there a public phone near here?
Hay uno a dos minutos de aquí.   There's one two minutes away from here.

Note: For reporting a loss or theft see page 76.

A la prueba

¿Qué hace este chico?

A) Echa una carta en el buzón.
B) Llama a cobro revertido.
C) Compra un sello para una postal.

Solución en la página 91.

◀ *Getting around* ▶

How to get into town

un asiento	seat	**coger**	to catch
un autocar	coach	**ir**	to go
una estación de	underground station	**lento**	slow
metro		**rápido**	fast
un plano	plan	**hay que**	it is necessary to;
cambiar	to change		you have to

¿Cómo se puede ir al centro?   How can one get into the town centre?
Se puede coger el metro.   You can take the underground.
¿Es directo?   Is it direct?
No, hay que cambiar.   No, you must change.

Signs and notices

la aduana	customs	**la cantina**	station buffet
el aparcamiento	parking	**la consigna**	left luggage office

la consigna (automática)	(automatic) luggage office		la taquilla	ticket office
un despacho de billetes	ticket office		el transbordo	change (of trains)
			alquilar	to hire
el destino	destination		aparcar	to park
un enlace	connection		empujar	to push
una entrada	entrance		estacionar	to park
el equipaje	luggage		informarse de	to find out about
un horario	timetable		prohibir	to forbid
la información	information		salir	to leave
la llegada	arrival		tirar	to pull
una maleta	suitcase		venir	to come
un mapa	map		con destino a (Madrid)	to (Madrid)
el mozo	porter			
una oficina de turismo	tourist information office		con retraso	late
			de pie	standing
la oficina de objetos perdidos	lost property office		(no) fumadores	(non) smoking
			libre	free
un pasajero	passenger		ocupado	taken; engaged
la reserva	reservation		procedente de (Barcelona)	from (Barcelona)
la sala de espera	waiting room			
la salida	departure		prohibido fumar	no smoking
la salida (de emergencia)	(emergency) exit		sentado	sitting

El tren con destino a Madrid sale dentro de cinco minutos.	The train to Madrid leaves in five minutes.
¡Atención! El tren procedénte de Barcelona llegará al andén tres dentro de dos minutos.	Attention! The train from Barcelona will arrive at platform 3 in two minutes.

Getting to a particular place

un aeropuerto	airport		un puerto	port
una bicicleta	bicycle		el tráfico	traffic
el centro	centre		el trayecto	route; journey
un coche	car		un tren	train
un conductor	driver		una visita	visit
un embotellamiento	traffic jam		conducir	to drive
una moto	motorbike		parar	to stop
un número	number		visitar	to visit
el peaje	toll		que	who; which

Perdone, ¿hay un autocar que va a Oviedo?	Excuse me, is there a coach which goes to Oviedo?
¿A qué hora hay un tren para Granada?	At what time is there a train to Granada?
¿Qué autobús va a la playa?	Which bus goes to the beach?
Hay que coger el número diecisiete.	You have to get the number 17.

Finding bus stops, toilets and platforms

un andén	platform		los servicios	toilets
una parada	stop		una vía	track

¿Hay una parada de autobús cerca de aquí?	Is there a bus stop near here?
Hay una parada enfrente del colegio.	There's a stop opposite the school.
¿Dónde están los servicios?	Where are the toilets?

Buying tickets

un billete	ticket		**un bonobús**	multisaver ticket
un billete de ida y vuelta	return ticket		**un kilómetro**	kilometre
			sacar	to get/purchase (a ticket)
un billete kilométrico	ticket costed by the distance travelled		**primera clase**	first class
un billete sencillo	single ticket		**segunda clase**	second class

Un billete de ida y vuelta para Tarragona, por favor.	A return ticket to Tarragona, please.
¿En qué clase?	Which class?
Segunda clase.	Second class.

Times of arrival and departure

un avión	plane		**aterrizar**	to land
una barca	small boat		**llegar**	to arrive
un barco	boat		**salir**	to leave
un retraso	delay		**volar**	to fly
un vuelo	flight		**por lo menos**	at least

¿A qué hora sale el tren para Alicante?	What time does the train for Alicante leave?
El expreso para Pamplona sale a las quince veinticinco.	The express for Pamplona leaves at 15.25.

A la prueba

How often does the train leave?

BLAU BLUE  **AZUL BLEU**

TURISTIC-TRAIN

Salidas cada 30 minutos aproximadamente desde las estaciones
ⓟ norte dirección ⓟ sur o viceversa

HORARIOS			
10.00 - 12.00 h. Temp. alta	10.00 - 13.00 h. Temp. baja	16.00 - 18.00 h. Temp. alta y baja	1/2 vuelta = 200 ptas. Vuelta completa = 400 ptas.
	18.00 - 20.30 h. Temp. baja	18.00 - 22.00 h. Temp. alta	Sólo vuelta completa = 400 pts. Desde el Lago

Ticket checks

comprobar	to check
perder	to lose
presentar	to show
ver	to see

Su billete, por favor.	Your ticket, please.
He perdido mi billete.	I've lost my ticket.

Solución en la página 91.

Note: For buying fuel, breakdowns and accidents see page 78.

THE WORLD OF WORK

◀ *Education and training* ▶

Future plans

el dinero	money	ser	to be
un examen	exam	tener éxito	to be successful
el éxito	success	tener suerte	to be lucky
el futuro	future	afortunado	fortunate; lucky
una profesión	profession	ambicioso	ambitious
un puesto	job	complicado	complicated
un resultado	result	interesante	interesting
el servicio militar	military service	inútil	useless
el trabajo	work	rico	rich
una universidad	university	así que	so
la vida	life	BUP	(Spanish equivalent of GCSE, but taken at 18)
deber	to be obliged to		
dejar el colegio	to leave school		
estudiar	to study	COU	(Spanish equivalent of A level, but taken at 20)
exigir	to require; demand		
ganar	to earn		
interesarse	to be interested in	cualquier cosa	anything
lograr	to get; to achieve	hay que	you have to
pagar bien/mal	to pay well/badly	más tarde	later
pensar	to think	quisiera	I'd like

¿Qué quieres hacer más tarde?	What do you want to do later?
Después de los exámenes, espero continuar en el colegio.	After the exams, I hope to carry on at school.
Más que nada, me gustaría empezar a trabajar.	More than anything, I'd like to start to work.
El año que viene, espero empezar COU.	Next year, I hope to start A levels.

◀ *Careers and employment* ▶

Travelling to work

durar	to last	volver	to return
llegar	to arrive	a veces	sometimes
salir	to leave	generalmente	generally
soler	to be in the habit of	normalmente	normally
venir	to come		

¿Cómo vienes/vas al colegio?	How do you come/go to school?
Suelo venir/ir en bicicleta.	I usually come/go by bike.
¿Coges el autobús para ir al trabajo?	Do you go to work by bus?
A veces voy a pie.	Sometimes I walk there.

Out of work

el desempleo	unemployment	**buscar**	to look for
un empleo	job	**estar en paro**	to be unemployed
un parado	someone who is unemployed	**de momento**	at the moment
el paro	unemployment	**duro**	hard

¿Qué hace tu hermano?	What does your brother do?
De momento está en paro.	At the moment he is unemployed.
Debe ser muy difícil.	It must be very difficult.
Sí, es duro.	Yes, it's hard.

Jobs and work experience

un(a) empleado/a	employee	**empezar**	to begin
una empresa	company	**emplear**	to employ
una fábrica	factory	**hacer**	to do
una oficina	office	**reunirse (con)**	to meet up (with)
el patrón	boss	**terminar**	to finish
una profesión	job	**trabajar**	to work
un salario	salary	**fácil**	easy
un sindicato	trade union	**peligroso**	dangerous
una tienda	shop	**nada**	nothing
la vida	life	**por**	per

¿En qué trabaja?	What job does (s)he do?
Trabaja en una fábrica.	(S)he works in a factory.
Trabaja cuarenta horas por semana.	(S)he works 40 hours per week.
¿Ya has tenido algún trabajo?	Have you already had a job?
Trabajé en una oficina durante una semana.	I worked in an office for one week.
Los fines de semana trabajo en una gasolinera.	At the weekends, I work in a petrol station.
Trabajo allí desde hace seis meses.	I've been working there for six months.

Spare time jobs

aburrido	boring	**un trabajo**	job
bien/mal pagado	well/badly paid	**ganar**	to earn
interesante	interesting	**pagar**	to pay
un(a) cajero/a	cashier	**repartir**	to deliver
un periódico	newspaper	**hacer de canguro**	to babysit
un sueldo	wage(s)	**sólo**	only

El fin de semana no trabajo.	I don't work at weekends.
Reparto periódicos todas las mañanas.	I deliver newspapers every morning.
He hecho de canguro bastante a menudo.	I've quite often babysat.
Me pagan tres libras por hora.	I get paid £3 per hour.
Lo encuentro interesante, pero bastante duro.	I find it interesting but quite hard.

Future plans

acostumbrarse	to get used to		vacilar	to hesitate
conseguir	•to get; to obtain		la carrera	career
continuar	to continue		un(a) estudiante	student
decidir	to decide		las notas	marks
dejar	to leave		los resultados	results
pasar	to spend		la suerte	luck
proteger	to protect		depende	it depends

¿Qué esperas hacer después de los exámenes?	What do you hope to do after the exams?
Me gustaría ir a la universidad.	I'd like to go to university.
Voy a dejar el colegio.	I'm going to leave school.

Jobs – yourself and your family

un abogado	lawyer		un(a) ingeniero/a	engineer
un(a) alumno/a	pupil		un(a) jefe/a	boss
una ama de casa	housewife		un marinero	sailor
un arquitecto	architect		un mecánico	mechanic
un artista	artist		un(a) mecanógrafo/a	typist
un(a) carnicero/a	butcher		un médico	doctor
un(a) cajero/a	cashier		una mujer policía	police officer
un(a) camarero/a	waiter/waitress			(female)
un cartero	postman		un(a) obrero/a	worker
un(a) cocinero/a	cook; chef		un(a) panadero/a	baker
una compañía	company		un(a) periodista	journalist
un(a) conductor/a	driver		un policía	police officer (male)
un(a) dentista	dentist		un(a) profesor/a	teacher
un(a) dependiente	salesman/woman;		un(a) secretario/a	secretary
(-ienta)	shop assistant		un soldado	soldier
un director	director; manager		un técnico	technician
un dueño	owner		un torero	bullfighter
un(a) enfermero/a	nurse		un trabajador	worker
un fontanero	plumber		ser	to be
un(a) granjero/a	farmer		como	like; as

Mi padre es enfermero.	My dad is a nurse.
Mi madre trabaja como programadora de ordenadores.	My mum works as a computer programmer.
Mi hermano quiere ser mecánico.	My brother wants to be a mechanic.
Mi madrastra ha sido dependienta desde hace tres años.	My stepmother has been a shop assistant for three years.

A la prueba

¿Cómo van estos estudiantes al colegio?
A) En tren
B) En autocar
C) En bicicleta
D) En coche

Solución en la página 91.

◀ *Advertising and publicity* ▶

Advertisements

un anuncio	advertisement	**engañar**	to deceive
una cartelera	entertainments guide	**esconder**	to hide
un dibujo	drawing	**parecer**	to seem
una imagen	picture	**prometer**	to promise
un letrero	sign; notice	**falso**	false
la moda	fashion	**magnífico**	magnificent
un póster	poster	**mejor**	better; best
la publicidad	publicity; advertising	**peor**	worse; worst
comprar	to buy	**prohibido**	forbidden

No me gusta nada esta foto.	I hate this photo.
Tampoco me gusta esta imagen.	I don't like this picture either.
Preferimos este anuncio.	We prefer this advertisement.

Publicity

una agencia de viajes	travel agency	**un informe**	piece of information; report
un agente	agent	**una lista**	list
un baile	dance	**un partido**	game; match
un concierto	concert	**un premio**	prize
un concurso	competition; quiz	**un siglo**	century
una corrida	bullfight	**una ventaja**	advantage
un día festivo	public holiday	**abrir**	to open; to switch on
una diversión	leisure activity	**celebrarse**	to happen
un espectáculo	show	**cerrar**	to close; to switch off
una fiesta	party; celebration	**empezar**	to begin
un folleto	brochure; leaflet	**necesario**	necessary
la información	information	**por persona**	per person

¡Grandes rebajas!	Big reductions!
Infórmense en la oficina de turismo.	Get your information at the tourist information office.

◀ *Communication* ▶

Telephone numbers

una guía telefónica	telephone directory	**marcar**	to dial
un número (de teléfono)	(telephone) number	**saber**	to know
		tener	to have
un prefijo	dialling code	**es**	it's; it is
un teléfono	telephone		

¿Cuál es tu número de teléfono?	What's your phone number?
Es el dos, treinta y cinco, veintisiete, quince.	It's 235.27.15.
¿Sabe cuál es el prefijo?	Do you know the dialling code?

Answer a telephone call

al habla	speaking		**diga / dígame**	hello (on the telephone)
		Señor Martínez.	Mr. Martínez speaking.	

Ask to speak to someone/Telephone messages

decir	to say	**dejar**	to leave
hablar	to speak	**estar comunicando**	to be engaged
llamar	to call	**tomar**	to take
poner	to put someone through	**volver a llamar**	to call (back)
		un recado	message
con	with	**despacio**	slowly
¿quién?	who?		

Buenos días, quisiera hablar con Juan, por favor.	Hello, I'd like to speak to Juan, please.
¿Está Pilar, por favor?	Is Pilar there, please?
¿Podría ponerme con la señorita López?	Could you put me through to Miss López?
Le pongo ahora.	I'm putting you through now.
¿De parte de quién?	Who's speaking?
¿Quiere dejar un recado?	Would you like to leave a message?
Dígale al director que el señor Pérez ha llamado.	Tell the manager that Mr. Pérez called.

Para mejorar la memoria 7

La memoria inmediata

Antes de hacer este ejercicio, repasa las páginas 31 a 47.
Estudia estos objetos durante dos minutos. Después, cierra el libro y, en menos de cuatro minutos, intenta escribir una lista de todos los objetos. El orden no es importante.
Compara tu lista con los dibujos.

Solución en la página 91.

THE INTERNATIONAL WORLD

◀ *Life in other countries and communities* ▶

Money and prices

un banco	bank	una oficina de	exchange office
un billete	(1,000 peseta) note	cambio	
(de mil pesetas)		un penique	penny
el cambio	change	una peseta (pta)	peseta
un cheque	cheque	una tarjeta de	credit card
un cheque de	traveller's cheque	crédito	
viaje/de viajero		cobrar	to charge
el dinero	money	costar	to cost
el IVA	VAT	valer	to be worth; to cost
una libra (esterlina)	pound (sterling)	incluido	included
una moneda	coin		

Quisiera cambiar veinte libras esterlinas.	I'd like to change £20.
¿Acepta usted cheques de viaje?	Do you accept traveller's cheques?
¿Tiene usted monedas de veinticinco pesetas para el teléfono?	Do you have any twenty-five peseta coins for the telephone?

◀ *Tourism* ▶

Talk about holidays

una estancia	stay	divertirse	to enjoy oneself
un hotel	hotel	estar de vacaciones	to be on holiday
un mes	month	pasar las vacaciones	to spend one's
un país	country		holidays
la playa	beach; seaside	tomar el sol	to sunbathe
el turismo	tourism	viajar	to travel
un(a) turista	tourist	zambullirse	to dive
las vacaciones	holidays	al extranjero	abroad
broncearse	to get a suntan	diferente	different
descansar	to rest	en casa de	at the home of

¿Has pasado unas buenas vacaciones?	Did you have a good holiday?
He ido al extranjero.	I've been abroad.
¿Adónde has ido?	Where did you go?
Fuimos a la costa.	We went to the seaside.

Describe a holiday

una brisa	breeze	un recuerdo	memory; souvenir
una casa	house	la vela	sailing
un chalet	villa	el windsurf	windsurfing
un ferri	ferry	alquilar	to rent; to hire
la gente	people	brillar	to shine

conocer	to get to know; to meet		**hacer camping**	to go camping
esquiar	to ski		**pasárselo bien**	to have a really good time
haber mucho/ poco que hacer	to be a lot/little to do		**estupendo**	great
hacer buen/mal tiempo	to be good/bad weather		**pasado**	last
hacer calor/frío	to be hot/cold		**ruidoso**	noisy
			en barco	by boat
			todos los días	every day

¿Dónde pasaste las vacaciones el año pasado?	Where did you spend your holidays last year?
Fui a Portugal con mi familia.	I went to Portugal with my family.
Nos quedamos en un hotel.	We stayed in a hotel.
Pasamos una semana allí.	We spent a week there.
Hizo buen tiempo todos los días.	The weather was good every day.
Vimos algunas cosas muy interesantes.	We saw some very interesting things.

Excursions and places of interest

el ambiente	atmosphere		**un rey**	king
una excursión	trip		**una sierra**	mountain range
un lago	lake		**un sitio**	place
un lugar	place		**recomendar**	to recommend
un monumento	monument		**bonito**	pretty
el paisaje	countryside; landscape		**histórico**	historic
un pueblo	small town; village		**típico**	typical
una reina	queen		**tranquilo**	quiet
			turístico	touristy

¿Fuiste en alguna excursión?	Did you go on any excursions?
Sí, visitamos unos castillos preciosos.	Yes, we visited some beautiful castles.
Vi todos los monumentos de Madrid.	I saw all the monuments in Madrid.
Nunca olvidaré estas vacaciones.	I will never forget these holidays.

◀ *Accommodation* ▶

Are rooms available?

un albergue juvenil	youth hostel		**la recepción**	reception
el alojamiento	accommodation		**un recepcionista**	receptionist
un apartamento	apartment; flat		**el terreno**	site
un camping	campsite		**una tienda de campaña**	tent
una caravana	caravan		**completo**	full
una habitación	room		**libre**	free
una llave	key		**lleno**	full
un parador	inn; hotel			

¿Tiene una habitación libre, por favor?	Do you have a room free, please?
Lo siento, pero el hotel está completo.	I'm sorry, but the hotel is full.
¿Tiene sitio para dos personas?	Do you have room for two people?

When and for how long

alojarse	to stay	**a partir de**	from
reservar	to reserve; to book	**del ... al ...**	from the ... to the ...
una reserva	booking	**hasta**	until
una semana	week	**para ... noches**	for ... nights

> **Muy señor mío / Muy señora mía**
> Quisiera reservar una habitación para dos personas en su hotel, del veintiocho de abril al dos de mayo.
> ¿Podría confirmar esta reserva, por favor?
> Le saluda atentamente:

What sort of room

el aire (acondicionado)	air conditioning	**con ducha**	with shower
los aseos	toilets	**doble**	double
un balcón	balcony	**individual**	single
un despertador	alarm clock	**lujoso**	luxurious
un lavabo	washbasin	**media pensión**	half board
una vista	view	**para una persona**	for one person
un wáter	toilet	**para dos personas**	for two people
con cama de matrimonio	with a double bed	**para una familia**	for a family
con cuarto de baño	with bathroom	**pensión completa**	full board
		privado	private
		ofrecer	to offer

¿Qué clase de habitación quería?	What sort of room did you want?
Quisiéramos una habitación con cuarto de baño.	We'd like a room with a bathroom.
A ser posible, me gustaría tener una habitación con vistas al mar.	If it is possible, I'd like a room with a sea-view.

Ask the cost

costar	to cost	**el precio**	price
incluido	included		

¿Cuánto es por persona?	How much is it per person?
¿Cuánto cuesta por noche?	How much does it cost per night?
¿Cuánto es la pensión completa?	How much is full board?

Accept or reject a room

aceptar	to accept	**algo**	something
gustarle a uno	to like	**de acuerdo**	that's O.K.
tomar	to take	**demasiado**	too

¿Tiene algo más barato?	Do you have anything cheaper?
De acuerdo, lo voy a tomar.	Fine, I'll take it.

Identify yourself

el apellido	surname		firmar	to sign
una ficha	form		llamarse	to be called
la firma	signature		rellenar	to fill in
un(a) hijo/a	son/daughter		británico	British
un huésped	guest		a nombre de	in the name of
un pasaporte	passport			

He reservado una habitación a nombre de Jones.	I've reserved a room in the name of Jones.
Se escribe J O N E S.	That is spelt J O N E S.
Somos cinco: mi señora, mi hijo, mis dos hijas, y yo.	There are five of us: my wife, my son, my two daughters, and I.

Ask about facilities

el aparcamiento	car park		un salón	lounge
un ascensor	lift		la sombra	shade
un bar	bar		una toalla	towel
una lavandería	laundry		aparcar	to park
la luz	light		funcionar	to work
el papel higiénico	toilet paper		tener	to have
una piscina	swimming pool		arriba	upstairs

Perdone, señor, ¿dónde están los servicios?	Excuse me, where are the toilets?
Están arriba.	They're upstairs.
¿Dónde está el restaurante, por favor?	Where is the restaurant, please?
En la planta baja.	On the ground floor.

Meal times

el almuerzo	lunch		el desayuno	breakfast
una cafetería	café		un restaurante	restaurant
la cena	dinner		abierto	open
el comedor	dining room		de ... a ...	from ... to ...
la comida	lunch; meal		servir	to serve

¿A qué hora es el desayuno?	What time is breakfast?
La comida se sirve de doce y media a tres.	Lunch is served from 12.30 until 3 o'clock.

Paying

la factura	bill		poder	to be able to
pagar	to pay		sólo	only

¿Me da la factura, por favor?	Please can I have my bill?
¿Cuánto es en total?	How much does it come to altogether?
Sólo tengo cheques de viaje.	I only have traveller's cheques.

Book accommodation

agradecer	to thank	**después (de)**	after; following
confirmar	to confirm	**en seguida**	at once
hospedarse	to stay	**por adelantado**	in advance
un depósito	deposit	**tarde**	late
un fax	fax	**temprano**	early

¿Puedo reservar una habitación para la noche del primero de agosto?	Can I book a room for the night of August 1st?
Le mandaré un depósito en seguida.	I'll send you a deposit straight away.
¿Podría enviarme un fax para confirmar la reserva?	Could you send me a fax to confirm the booking?
Le saluda atentamente	Yours faithfully

Estimada señora,
Después de nuestra conversación telefónica, le escribo para confirmar la reserva de una habitación doble para la noche del treinta de julio.
¿Podría enviarme una lista de precios y un poco de información sobre el hotel?
Le saluda atentamente:

Note: For youth hostels and campsites see page 86.

A la prueba

¿Dónde pasaste las vacaciones el año pasado?

Solución en la página 91.

◀ *The wider world* ▶

Understand names of countries

América del Sur	South America		**una frontera**	frontier; border
Australia	Australia		**el mundo**	world
el Canadá	Canada		**un país**	country
los Estados Unidos	U.S.A.		**la tierra**	earth
la bandera	flag		**ser de**	to be from

For European countries, see page 10.

Pasé las vacaciones de Pascua en Suiza.	I spent the Easter holidays in Switzerland.
Me gustaría mucho ir a los Estados Unidos.	I'd really like to go to the U.S.A.
Nunca he ido al Canadá.	I've never been to Canada.

Nationalities and languages

alemán	German		**griego**	Greek
americano	American		**holandés**	Dutch
australiano	Australian		**inglés**	English
austriaco	Austrian		**irlandés**	Irish
belga	Belgian		**italiano**	Italian
danés	Danish		**portugués**	Portuguese
escocés	Scottish		**sudamericano**	South American
español	Spanish		**sueco**	Swedish
finlandés	Finnish		**suizo**	Swiss
francés	French		**la nacionalidad**	nationality
galés	Welsh			

Mi padre es italiano.	My father is Italian.
Mi madre es española.	My mother is Spanish.
Hablo portugués.	I speak Portuguese.

Spanish geography

Andalucía	Andalusia		**el País Vasco**	Basque Country
Cataluña	Catalonia		**los Pirineos**	Pyrenees
Costa Brava	Costa Brava		**andaluz**	from Andalusia
Costa Cantábrica	Costa Cantábrica		**castellano**	Castilian
Costa del Sol	Costa del Sol		**catalán**	Catalan
Costa Verde	Costa Verde		**gallego**	from Galicia
Galicia	Galicia		**mediterráneo**	Mediterranean

◀ *Examination Spanish* ▶

The list below contains the words which will be used in instructions and questions in your Spanish exam. Make sure that you know them. This will make you faster and more successful!

Rubrics and Instructions

abre	open	**imagina**	imagine
añade	add	**indica con una equis**	show with a cross; put a cross
busca en el diccionario	look up in the dictionary	**indica con una marca**	show with a tick; put a tick
cambia (los detalles)	change (the details)	**justifica tu opinión**	justify your opinion
cierra	close	**lee**	read
compara	compare	**marca con una equis**	show with a cross; mark with a cross
completa	complete		
contesta (las preguntas)	answer (the questions)	**menciona**	mention
convence	convince	**mira**	look at
copia	copy	**opinar**	to give an opinion
corresponder a	to correspond to	**pide**	ask for
cubrir	to cover	**pon en orden**	put in the right order
da razones	give reasons	**pon una equis/ una marca en la casilla correcta**	put a cross/tick in the right box
da tu opinión sobre	give your opinion on		
decide	decide		
describe	describe	**pon una equis/una marca en todas las casillas correctas**	put a cross/tick in all the right boxes
detalle	detail		
dibuja	draw		
diseña	draw; sketch	**prepara**	prepare
empareja	match; pair up	**prepara una presentación oral**	prepare a talk
encuentra	find		
escribe el número/ la letra/una lista	write the number/ the letter/a list	**rellena la tabla/los espacios/el formulario**	fill in the grid/the spaces/the form
escoge	choose		
elegir	to choose	**significar**	to mean
escucha (la cinta)	listen to (the tape)	**subraya**	underline
estudia (el cuadro)	study (the grid)	**sugiere**	suggest
explica	explain	**un anuncio**	advertisement
habla	speak	**una conversación**	conversation
haz un anuncio	make up an advertisement	**ejemplo**	example
		un ejercicio	exercise
haz una comparación	compare	**espacio**	space
		una explicación	explanation
haz un diálogo	make up a conversation	**el formulario**	form
		un póster	poster
haz una entrevista	carry out an interview	**una pregunta**	question
		¿a qué hora?	what time?
haz una lista	make a list	**¿cierto o falso?**	true or false?
haz el papel de	play the part of	**¿cómo?**	how?
haz preguntas	ask questions	**¿cómo es/son?**	what is it/are they like?
haz un resumen	summarise		

¿cuál/cuáles?	which?	¿estás de acuerdo?	do you agree?
¿cuál es tu actitud hacia ...?	what is your attitude towards ...?	¿qué conclusiones sacas?	what conclusions can you draw?
¿cuáles son las diferencias entre ...?	what are the differences between ...?	¿qué diferencias hay entre ..?	what differences are there between ...?
		¿qué significa/ significan?	what does it/do they mean?
¿cuáles son las ventajas/los inconvenientes?	what are the advantages/ disadvantages?	¿quién/quiénes?	who?
¿cuándo?	when?	de	of
¿cuánto/cuántos?	how much/how many?	según (la información)	according to (the information)
¿dónde/adónde?	where/where to?	verdad/mentira/ no se sabe	true/false/don't know

Here are the most common exam instructions:

Aquí hay unas notas para ayudarte.	Here are some notes to help you.
¿Cómo describirías a ...?	How would you describe ...?
Completa las siguientes frases.	Complete the following phrases.
Completa los detalles.	Complete the details.
Contesta en español.	Answer in Spanish.
Copia el nombre en la casilla adecuada.	Copy the name in the appropriate box.
Da los siguientes detalles.	Give the following details.
¿De qué se trata esta conversación?	What is this conversation about?
Empareja cada párrafo con un resumen.	Match each paragraph to a summary.
Escoge la frase correcta.	Choose the correct phrase.
Escribe aproximadamente ... palabras.	Write approximately ... words.
Escribe debajo de los dibujos.	Write underneath the pictures.
Escribe dos cosas.	Write two things.
Escribe el texto de un folleto.	Write the text for a leaflet.
Escribe la palabra que falta.	Write in the missing word.
Escribe para hacer una reserva.	Write to make a booking.
Escribe una carta contestando las preguntas.	Write a letter answering the questions.
Escribe una lista.	Write a list.
Escribe unas notas en español.	Write some notes in Spanish.
Escucha los pronósticos del tiempo.	Listen to the weather forecasts.
Explica lo que es ...	Explain what is ...
Explica tu decisión.	Explain your decision.
Hay que contestar según las instrucciones.	Answer according to the instructions.
Lee este artículo.	Read this article.
Llena el espacio con una palabra de la lista.	Fill the gap with a word from the list.
Menciona los siguientes puntos.	Mention the following points.
Para cada pregunta pon una X en la casilla correcta.	For each question put a cross in the right box.
Pon la letra adecuada.	Put in the appropriate letter.
Rellena los espacios.	Fill in the gaps.
Subraya la palabra correcta.	Underline the correct word.

HIGHER TIER

EVERYDAY ACTIVITIES

◀ *Language of the classroom* ▶

Explain a word/How is it pronounced?

una cosa	thing		**¿cómo?**	how?
el sentido	meaning		**pronunciar(se)**	to pronounce
explicar	to explain			

¿Podría usted explicarme el sentido de esta palabra?	Could you explain the meaning of this word to me?
¿Qué quiere decir eso?	What does that mean?
Esa cosa allí, ¿cómo se llama?	What's that thing there called?
¿Cómo se pronuncia eso?	How is that pronounced?

◀ *School* ▶

Learning languages

defenderse	to get by		**saber**	to know
dominar	to speak fluently		**un idioma**	language

¿Desde cuándo estudias español?	How long have you been learning Spanish?
Estudio español desde hace cinco años.	I've been learning Spanish for five years.
¿Sabes algún otro idioma extranjero?	Do you know any other foreign languages?
He estudiado alemán durante casi tres años.	I've studied German for nearly three years.
Me defiendo en francés.	I get by in French.
Domino el español.	I speak Spanish fluently.

School timetables

el año académico	school year		**demasiado**	too; too much; too many
un trimestre	term		**obligatorio**	compulsory

Para mí, el mejor trimestre es el segundo.	For me, the best term is the second one.
En mi opinión, hay demasiadas asignaturas.	In my opinion, there are too many subjects.
Creo que el francés no debe ser obligatorio.	I think that French should not be compulsory.
¿Qué opina usted?	What do you think about it?
A lo mejor tienes razón.	Perhaps you're right.

School rules

el derecho	the right		**llevar**	to wear
una regla	rule		**a favor**	for
un uniforme	uniform		**en contra**	against
absurdo	stupid		**totalmente**	completely
ridículo	ridiculous			

¿Estás a favor o en contra del uniforme obligatorio en el colegio?	Are you for or against compulsory uniform at school?
Estoy más bien a favor, porque es más fácil y más barato.	I'm rather for it, because it's easier and cheaper.
Me parece totalmente ridículo.	I find it completely ridiculous.
Es una buena idea tener reglas.	It's a good idea to have rules.
Hay algunas reglas absurdas.	There are some stupid rules.

Different types of school

la educación	education		**la mayor parte**	most
la enseñanza	teaching		**de segunda**	secondary
la escolaridad	schooling		**enseñanza**	
una guardería infantil	nursery school		**mixto**	mixed
			primario	primary
un instituto para COU	6th form college		**privado**	private
			religioso	religious

Casi todos los niños españoles van a una guardería infantil a partir de los cuatro años.	Nearly all Spanish children go to a nursery school from the age of four.
Hay algunos colegios privados en España.	There are some private schools in Spain.
La escolaridad es obligatoria de cinco a dieciséis años.	Schooling is compulsory from the age of 5 to 16.

◀ *Home life* ▶

Typical meals, meal times and eating habits

abundante	copious		**pesado**	heavy
dulce	sweet		**salado**	salty; savoury
ligero	light		**soler**	to be in the habit of

En nuestra casa, el desayuno es una comida bastante ligera.	In our house, breakfast is quite a light meal.
Normalmente, la comida es bastante abundante.	Usually, dinner is quite substantial.
Normalmente, prefiero los platos salados.	Normally, I prefer savoury dishes.
¿No te gustan las bebidas dulces?	Don't you like sweet drinks?
Solemos cenar bastante tarde.	We usually have dinner quite late.

Helping around the house

un cazo	saucepan		**barrer**	to brush; sweep
el cubo de basura	dustbin		**echar una mano**	to give a hand
una papelera	waste paper bin		**ir a buscar**	to look for
una sartén	(frying) pan		**sacar**	to take out
(lavar) la vajilla	(to do) the washing up		**secar**	to (wipe) dry
			usar	to use

¿Puedo echar una mano?	Can I give you a hand?
¿Podrías ayudarme?	Could you help me?
¿Quieres fregar los cazos?	Will you wash up the pans?
Mete los platos en el fregadero, por favor.	Put the dishes in the sink, please.

How members of the family help at home

cocinar	to cook		**el césped**	lawn
cortar la hierba	to cut the grass		**justo**	fair
poner la mesa	to set the table		**nada**	nothing
quitar la mesa	to clear the table		**todo**	everything

En nuestra casa, es mi madre la que hace todo.	In our house, it's my mother who does everything.
Siempre es mi padre el que hace los arreglos.	It's always my dad who does the odd jobs.
Normalmente, yo seco los platos.	Usually, I dry the dishes.
Ayer, por ejemplo, quité la mesa.	Yesterday, for example, I cleared the table.
¿Crees que eso es justo?	Do you think that that is fair?
Mi hermano no hace nada.	My brother doesn't do anything.

Say if you share a room

compartir	to share		**propio**	own
tener que	to have to		**sólo**	only
la suerte	luck			

Tengo que compartir un dormitorio	I have to share a bedroom.
Tengo mi propia habitación.	I have my own room.
¡Qué suerte tienes!	How lucky you are!
Me gustaría tener un dormitorio sólo para mí.	I'd really like to have a room just for me.
No me gusta compartir con mi hermana.	I don't like sharing with my sister.

◀ *Media* ▶

A la prueba

Para leer

En una revista, lees este resumen de un nuevo libro. Explica de qué se trata a un amigo que no entiende español.

Pequeño País No 664 21/8/94

Para leer

Billy y el vestido rosa. Todo comenzó una mañana cuando su madre le puso para ir al colegio un sorprendente vestido rosa. Billy era incapaz de reaccionar. ¿Qué hacía él vestido así? Además nadie parecía darse cuenta del cambio. Nadie excepto él. Ese día, el mas largo de su vida, y tras no pocos percances escolares, Billy empezó a darse cuenta de las ventajas y los inconvenientes de ser chica. Un libro de Alfaguara Infantil.

Solución en la página 91.

Narrate a theme or plot of a book

un cuento	story
un escritor	author; writer
el héroe	hero
la heroina	heroine
una historia	story
una novela	novel
un novelista	novelista
un personaje	character
un protagonista	main character
acabar de	to have just
comenzar por	to begin by
emocionante	exciting
principal	main; principal
al final	at the end
al principio	at the start
se trataba de	it was about

¿Te gusta leer?	Do you like reading?
Sí, acabo de leer una novela muy buena.	Yes, I've just read a very good novel.
¿De qué se trataba?	What was it about?
Es un cuento emocionante.	It's an exciting story.

Narrate a simple item of news

amenazar	to threaten	**una guerra**	war
asesinar	to murder; to assassinate	**una huelga**	strike
		un juez	judge
castigar	to punish	**un ladrón**	thief
cometer	to commit	**una ley**	law
ganar	to beat; to win	**la libertad**	freedom; liberty
huir	to flee	**una manifestación**	show; demonstration
luchar	to fight; to struggle	**las noticias**	news
matar	to kill	**la paz**	peace
oír	to hear	**un telediario**	TV news programme
pasar	to happen	**un terrorista**	terrorist
perder	to lose	**ha habido**	there has been
secuestrar	to kidnap; to hijack	**habrá**	there will be
un atraco	holdup; robbery	**hubo**	there was
la cárcel	prison	**parece que**	it seems that
el delito	crime; offence	**reciente**	recent
el gobierno	government	**según**	according to

¿Has oído lo que pasó ayer?	Have you heard what happened yesterday?
Vi las noticias en la televisión.	I saw the news on TV.
Habrá huelgas en todas partes.	There will soon be strikes everywhere.

| Según el periódico, ha habido un terrible accidente. | According to the newspaper, there has been a terrible accident. |
| España ganó a Inglaterra. | Spain beat England. |

Newspapers, magazines, books, TV programmes, radio, music and performers

un artículo	article	divertido	amusing; funny
un cambio	change	excluido	excluded
un(a) cantante	singer	fatal	awful
una esperanza	hope	último	last; latest
una excavación	dig; search	confiar en	to confide in
la tierra	earth	fiarse de	to trust
auténtico	real; true	odiar	to hate

¿Has oído el último disco de ....?	Have you heard the latest record by ...?
¿Quién es tu cantante preferida?	Who is your favourite female singer?
¿Viste el programa en la televisión anoche?	Did you see the programme on TV last night?
¿Qué te pareció?	What did you think of it?
Fue malísimo.	It was awful.
Me gustó muchísimo.	I liked it a lot.

A la prueba

Esta noche en la tele
Lee estos artículos y, sin consultar el diccionario, contesta las siguientes preguntas.

1 ¿A qué hora empieza el programa que intenta localizar a gente desaparecida?
2 ¿En qué canal hay un programa para los amantes de la naturaleza?
3 ¿Cómo se llama el programa que trata de la historia reciente de España?

SUGERENCIAS

13.45 / Tele 5

Fórmula 1

Tele 5 continúa retransmitiendo todas las carreras del Campeonato del Mundo de Fórmula 1. Hoy conecta en directo con Budapest para ofrecer, desde el circuito de Hungarorin, el Gran Premio de Hungría. Damon Hill (Williams) y Michael Schumacher (Benetton) parten como favoritos.

El piloto de Williams Damon Hill.

15.00 / Canal +

Halcones en el desierto

Este es el título del nuevo documental que estrena Canal +, perteneciente al catálogo de National Geographic. *Halcones en el desierto* muestra, durante 30 minutos, las principales características

físicas y de comportamiento del halcón Harris, que habita el desierto de Sonora, en el noroeste de México. El vuelo de estos animales, que llegan a alcanzar velocidades de 320 kilómetros por hora, y las encarnizadas batallas que mantienen con algunos de sus peores enemigos, como las serpientes de cascabel y las lechuzas, son algunos de los aspectos tratados en el reportaje.

▶ *Quién sabe dónde*
21.30, TVE-1

Paco Lobatón presenta, en *Quién sabe dónde*, nuevos casos de personas que se encuentran en paradero desconocido.

19.00 / La 2

Cuéntame cómo pasó

El programa *Cuéntame cómo pasó* trata hoy de la revolución que supuso la implantación de la nevera en los hogares españoles de los años cincuenta. Gloria Lasso, cuyas canciones estaban en pleno apogeo en aquellos años, interpretará fragmentos de sus canciones favoritas. También se recordará lo que sucedía en el mundo en una época en que las amas de casa españolas dejaron de depender de una barra de hielo.

Solución en la página 91.

◀ *Health and fitness* ▶

Arrange to consult a doctor, dentist or chemist

una clínica	clinic	consultar	to consult
la consulta	surgery	pedir hora	to ask for an appointment
un dentista	dentist		
un(a) farmacéutico/a	chemist	sentirse	to feel
un médico	doctor	ocupado	busy
la salud	health	urgente	urgent

Me siento muy mal.	I feel really ill.
Creo que debería ir a ver al médico.	I think I ought to go and see the doctor.
¿Puedo pedir hora con el dentista, por favor?	Can I make an appointment with the dentist, please?
Lo siento, pero hoy está ocupado todo el día.	I'm sorry, but he's busy all day today.
Es urgente.	It's urgent.
Tengo que verle hoy.	I must see him today.
Entonces, ¿podría usted venir esta tarde a las cinco y media?	Could you come this afternoon at 5.30?

At a doctor's, dentist's or chemist's

el algodón	cotton wool	la sangre	blood
una aspirina	aspirin	el síntoma	symptom
la boca	mouth	una tirita	plaster
un consejo	piece of advice	el tobillo	ankle
un corte	cut	la tos	cough
una crema	cream	el tratamiento	treatment
una cucharada	spoonful	un tubo	tube
una cura	cure	una venda	dressing
la diarrea	diarrhoea	aconsejar	to advise
el esparadrapo	sticking plaster	ahogarse	to drown
la fiebre	temperature	cortar(se)	to cut (oneself)
la gripe	influenza; flu	descansar	to rest
una herida	injury	estar constipado	to have a cold
el hombro	shoulder	morir	to die
una inyección	injection	pasar	to happen
el jarabe	linctus	quemarse	to burn oneself
el labio	lip	romperse	to break
el mareo	travel sickness; seasickness	sufrir	to suffer
		temblar	to tremble; to shiver
un medicamento	medicine	torcerse	to twist
la medicina	medicine	tratar	to treat
la mejilla	cheek	vomitar	to be sick
una operación	operation	grave	serious
una pastilla	tablet	muerto	dead
la piel	skin	sano	healthy
una píldora	pill	doctor	(how you address a doctor)
una receta	prescription		
un remedio	remedy; cure		

¿Qué le ha pasado?	What has happened?
Me he roto el brazo.	I've broken my arm.
He pasado demasiado tiempo al sol.	I spent too much time in the sun.
¿Tiene usted fiebre?	Have you got a temperature?
Me he torcido el tobillo.	I've twisted my ankle.
Le aconsejo ir a la cama y descansar.	I advise you to go to bed and rest.
Voy a darle una receta.	I'll give you a prescription.

Healthy and unhealthy lifestyles

la adicción	addiction		en forma	in good shape
el alcohol	alcohol		equilibrado	balanced
una caloría	calorie		grueso	fat
una droga	drug		abstenerse de	to avoid
un régimen	diet		entrenarse	to train
el sueño	sleep		evitar	to avoid
el tabaco	tobacco		fumar	to smoke
una vitamina	vitamin		practicar un deporte	to practise a sport
delgado	thin		seguir	to follow

Yo nunca tomaría drogas.	I'd never take drugs.
Es mejor seguir un régimen equilibrado.	It's best to follow a balanced diet.
¿Qué haces para mantenerte en forma?	What do you do to stay in good shape?
No debe fumar.	You shouldn't smoke.

◄ *Food* ►

React to offers of food or drink, giving reasons

un caracol	snail		apetitoso	appetising
una garrafa	carafe		probar	to try
un mejillón	mussel		medio hecho	medium (of meat)
un olor	smell		muy hecho	well done (of meat)
un pulpo	octopus		poco hecho	rare (of meat)
el sabor	taste		con mucho gusto	with pleasure
una sardina	sardine		me es igual	I don't mind
alérgico	allergic		ya basta	that's enough

¿Un poco más de cordero?	A little more lamb?
¿Quiere repetir?	Do you want some more?
No gracias, ya basta.	No thanks, that's enough.
Soy alérgico a los mejillones.	I'm allergic to mussels.
Nunca he probado la trucha con almendras.	I've never tasted trout with almonds.
Estoy tomando medicamentos y no puedo beber alcohol.	I'm taking medication and I can't drink alcohol.

Appreciation and compliments

el cocinero	chef; cook		felicitaciones	(my) compliments
la salsa	sauce; gravy		inolvidable	unforgettable
felicitar	to congratulate		sobre todo	above all
enhorabuena	congratulations			

Sobre todo me ha gustado el postre.   I especially liked the dessert.
Felicitaciones al cocinero.   My compliments to the chef.
Muchas gracias por una cena inolvidable.   Many thanks for an unforgettable dinner.

Ask for more or say that you have had enough

queda	there is left	**repetir**	to take some more

¿Queda cordero?   Is there any lamb left?
Voy a repetir, con mucho gusto.   I'll have some more with pleasure.
Me encantan las patatas fritas, ¿puedo servirme más, por favor?   I love the chips, can I have some more, please?
¿Podría traernos otra garrafa de agua?   Could you bring us another carafe of water?
He comido demasiado (bastante).   I've already eaten too much (enough).
Así está bien, gracias.   That's fine as it is, thanks.

Ask for a table/State preference for seating

una persona	person	**la parte de no fumadores**	non-smoking area
reservar	to reserve; to book		
dentro	inside	**una terraza**	terrace
fuera	outside		

¿Cuántos son ustedes?   How many of you are there?
Somos cinco.   There are five of us.
¿Tiene una mesa para una persona?   Do you have a table for one?
¿Podemos sentarnos en una mesa en la terraza?   Can we have a table on the terrace?
Preferiría una mesa dentro.   I'd prefer a table inside.
Nos gustaría estar en la parte de no fumadores.   We'd like to be in the non-smoking area.

Complain, giving reasons

el (la) director/a	manager	**lento**	slow
el (la) dueño/a	owner	**satisfecho**	satisfied
una queja	complaint	**protestar**	to protest
inadmisible	unacceptable	**completamente**	entirely

Quisiera hablar con el director.   I'd like to talk to the manager.
No hemos pedido sidra.   We didn't order any cider.
Pedí un filete poco hecho y me lo han traído bien hecho.   I ordered a rare steak and they have brought me one which is well-done.
El servicio fue muy lento.   The service was very slow.
No estoy nada satisfecho.   I'm not at all satisfied.
Nos metieron en la parte de fumadores.   We were put in the smoking section.

PERSONAL AND SOCIAL LIFE

◀ *Self, family and friends* ▶

State, and understand others stating gender and marital status

una esposa	wife	de edad	aged
una hermanastra	stepsister	divorciado	divorced
un hermanastro	stepbrother	femenino	feminine
una madrastra	stepmother	masculino	masculine
el nacimiento	birth	mayor	elder
un padrastro	stepfather	menor	younger
el sexo	sex	prometido	engaged
una viuda	widow	separado	separated
un viudo	widower	soltero	single; unmarried
casado	married	casarse	to marry

Mi hermana mayor tiene dos hijos, un chico de tres años y una chica de ocho meses.	My elder sister has two children, a boy of three and a daughter of eight months.
Mi hermano es soltero.	My brother is not married.
Mis padres son divorciados desde hace dos años.	My parents have been divorced for two years.

Spell out names, streets and towns

una avenida	avenue	deletrear	to spell
el domicilio	home address		

Mi dirección es Avenida Lombardo 23.	My address is 23, Lombardo Avenue.
Vivo en un pequeño pueblo que se llama Adzeneta.	I live in a small village called Adzeneta.
¿Podrías deletrear el nombre del pueblo?	Could you spell the name of the village?

Describe character and personality

activo	active	nervioso	nervous; nervy
antipático	unpleasant	optimista	optimistic
cariñoso	gentle; caring	pesimista	pessimistic
celoso	jealous	raro	odd; strange
desagradable	disagreeable	testarudo	stubborn
dinámico	dynamic; energetic	travieso	naughty
educado	educated; polite	vago	idle
egoísta	selfish	contar con	to count on
encantador	charming	fastidiar	to annoy
(in)feliz	(un)happy	portarse bien	to be well behaved
honesto	honest	el carácter	character
insoportable	unbearable	tan	so

¿Qué te ha parecido la amiga de Pedro?	How did you find Pedro's girl friend?		
Me pareció bastante antipática.	I found her rather unpleasant.		
Martina es de confianza, puedes contar con ella.	Martina is very reliable, you can count on her.		
Marcos me fastidia mucho. Siempre es tan testarudo.	Marcos really gets on my nerves. He's always so stubborn.		

Express feelings about others

entenderse	to get on together		pobre	poor
llevarse bien/mal	to get on well/badly		raro	strange
parecer	to seem; to appear		responsable	responsible
preocuparse	to worry		sorprendente	surprising
respetar	to respect		naturalmente	naturally
tener éxito	to be successful		perfectamente	perfectly
elegante	elegant		una sonrisa	smile
inquieto	worried		un(a) vecino/a	neighbour
listo	clever		cada uno	each one
peor	worse; worst			

¿Te entiendes bien con tus padres?	Do you get on well with your parents?
Me llevo mal con mi madrastra.	I get on badly with my stepmother.
¿Qué piensa usted de mi padrastro?	What do you think of my stepfather?
Me parece una persona muy simpática.	He seems a very kind person to me.

◄ *Free time, holidays and special occasions* ►

Hobbies, interests and leisure activities

un balón	ball (large)		una ópera	opera
un(a) campeón/-eona	champion		una pelota	ball (small)
			ir a pasear	to go for a walk
un(a) ciclista	cyclist		ir de paseo	to go for a walk
el cricket	cricket		sólo	only
un(a) jugador/a	player			

Sobre todo me gusta ir a pasear en el campo.	Above all, I like walking in the country.
A mi hermano pequeño le encanta jugar con el balón.	My little brother loves playing ball.
En mi opinión, el mejor deporte del mundo es el cricket.	In my opinion, the best sport in the world is cricket.
Mi padre va mucho a la ópera.	My dad goes to the opera a lot.

Clubs

un abono	club subscription	abonarse a	to subscribe to
una actividad	activity	apreciar	to appreciate
el ballet	ballet	asistir a	to attend; to be present at
el billar americano	pool		
el billar inglés	snooker	frecuentar	to frequent; to go somewhere regularly
una charla	talk		
una reunión	meeting	participar en	to take part in
una sociedad	society	tener tiempo para	to have time to

¿Eres socio de algún club?	Are you a member of any club?
Sí, el fin de semana asisto a las reuniones de una sociedad musical.	Yes, at weekends I attend the meetings of a musical society.
La semana pasada fui a una conferencia excelente sobre el jazz moderno.	Last week I went to an excellent lecture on modern jazz.
Voy todas las semanas a un club de jóvenes.	I go to a youth club every week.

Holidays and activities

un carrete	film (for a camera)	acordarse	to remember
un guía	guide	broncearse	to get a suntan
una guía	guide-book	marcharse	to go away
el mundo	world	recordar	to remember
un parque zoológico	zoo	veranear	to spend the summer holidays
el veraneante	holidaymaker	cada	each; every

Salgo poco, ya que no tengo tiempo con todos mis deberes.	I don't go out much as I don't have the time with all my homework.
El verano pasado fui a España y me broncé.	Last summer I went to Spain and got a suntan.
El próximo año, haremos turismo en el norte de España.	Next year, we'll go touring in the north of Spain.
Cuando tenga un día de vacaciones, iré al nuevo parque de atracciones.	When I have a day's holiday, I'll go to the new theme park.

Sporting events

un cartel	poster	un partido	match
el estadio	sports ground	aburrirse	to get bored
una lástima	pity	malísimo	very bad; awful

El sábado pasado, fui a una corrida de toros.	Last Saturday, I went to see a bullfight.
Me aburrí.	I was bored.
¡Qué lástima!	What a pity!
Me gusta hacer todo tipo de deporte.	I like taking part in all types of sports.
En mi opinión, el partido era malísimo.	In my opinion, the game was awful.

Information about excursions and visits

una agencia de viajes	travel agency		un valle	valley
una oficina de turismo	tourist information office		medieval	medieval
			no me importa	I don't mind

¿Tiene folletos sobre las excursiones al valle de Arán?	Do you have any leaflets about excursions to the Aran valley?
¿Cuándo quiere ir?	When would you like to go?
No me importa.	I don't mind.
Podría ir a visitar el castillo medieval.	You could go and visit the medieval castle.

Discuss preferences and alternatives for going out

los anuncios breves	small ads		descansar	to rest
una obra de teatro	play		sugerir	to suggest
un subtítulo	sub-title		en cualquier parte	anywhere
un título	title		juntos	together

Ponen una buena película en el centro, ¿vamos a verla juntos?	There's a good film in town, shall we go and see it together?
Es en versión original, con subtítulos en español.	It's with the original soundtrack and Spanish sub-titles.
Me gustaría más ir a ver una obra de teatro.	I'd rather go and see a play.
¿Por qué no nos quedamos en casa a ver la tele?	Why don't we stay at home to watch TV?

Money

gastar	to spend		un aumento	increase; rise
pedir prestado	to borrow		un presupuesto	budget
recibir	to receive		pelado	broke; hard up

Estoy pelado y no podré salir esta noche.	I'm broke and I won't be able to go out this evening.
He gastado todo mi dinero en ropa.	I've spent all my money on clothes.
Sólo me quedan cincuenta pesetas.	I've only got fifty pesetas left.
Sólo tengo doscientas pesetas.	I've only got 200 pesetas.
Quizás podría pedirle dinero prestado a mi hermano.	Perhaps I could borrow some money from my brother.
Debo pedir un aumento.	I must ask for an increase.
Nunca tengo bastante dinero.	I've never got enough money.

◀ *Personal relationships and social activities* ▶

Ask permission to do things

aparcar	to park	el maquillaje	make-up
conducir	to drive	el permiso	permission
grabar	to record	un vídeo	video
permitir	to allow	no hay de qué	not at all
prohibir	to forbid	prohibido	forbidden to
tirar	to throw	sírvete; sírvase	help yourself

¿Podría usar el vídeo para grabar un programa?	Could I use the video to record a programme?
¿Puedo ponerme maquillaje?	Can I wear make-up?
No, no está permitido en el colegio.	No, it's not allowed at school.
¿Está bien?	Is it all right?
¿Se puede fumar aquí?	Can one smoke here?
No, está prohibido.	No, it's forbidden.
¿Puedo salir?	May I go out?

Apologise

asegurar	to assure	preocuparse	to worry
disculparse	to apologise	la culpa	fault; blame
enfadarse	to get angry	adrede	on purpose
molestar	to disturb; to inconvenience	¡Dios mío!	my God!
		¡Madre mía!	oh dear!
perdonar	to forgive		

Perdone, no debería haberme enfadado.	Forgive me, I shouldn't have lost my temper.
Lo siento, la culpa ha sido mía.	I'm sorry, it was my fault.
Le aseguro que no lo he hecho adrede.	I assure you that I didn't do it on purpose.
No se preocupe, fue un accidente.	Don't worry, it was an accident.

Discuss your problems

aguantar	to stand; to put up with	mentir	to lie
arreglárselas	to get by	parecerle bien a uno	to approve of
asombrar	to astonish	protestar	to protest
crear	to create	respetar	to respect
creer	to believe	un adolescente	adolescent
criticar	to criticise	el alquiler	rent
dar vergüenza	to embarrass; to bother	la carrera	career
		una catástrofe	catastrophe
decir mentiras	to tell lies	la confianza	confidence
discutir	to quarrel; to argue	una crisis	crisis
estar harto de	to be fed up with	una pandilla	gang (of friends)
hablar de	to discuss	la política	politics
insultar	to insult	una solución	solution
		asombroso	amazing

desilusionado	disappointed	a pesar de	in spite of
enfadado	angry; annoyed	gracias a	thanks to
económico	economic		
evidente	·obvious		

Estoy harto de todo.	I'm fed up with everything.
Discuto a menudo con mis padres.	I often quarrel with my parents.
La gente mayor no entiende a los adolescentes.	Old people don't understand adolescents.
Mi madre siempre se queja de mí.	My mother is always complaining about me.
¿Qué me aconsejas hacer?	What do you advise me to do?

◀ *Arranging a meeting or activity* ▶

Entertainment options

un baile	·dance; a ball	**tener ganas de**	to feel like; to be dying to
el judo	judo		

¿Se puede practicar el judo aquí?	Can you do judo here?
¿Hay un partido de rugby el domingo próximo?	Is there a rugby match next Sunday?
Tengo ganas de ir a la discoteca, ¿es posible?	I feel like going to a disco: is that possible?
Podríamos escuchar música, si prefieres.	We could listen to music if you prefer.

Negotiate a meeting

depender	to depend	**ciertamente**	certainly
impedir	to prevent	**de nuevo**	again
quedar	to arrange to meet	**encantado**	delighted
una intención	intention	**sin duda**	without doubt
a punto de	about to; on the point of	**temprano**	early

Estoy a punto de ir al centro: ¿quieres acompañarme?	I'm just about to go into town: do you want to come with me?
No puedo salir esta noche.	I can't go out tonight.
De acuerdo, pero tendré que volver a casa temprano.	OK, but I must be home early.
¿Por qué no nos vemos mañana por la mañana?	Shall we see each other tomorrow morning?

◀ *Leisure and entertainment* ▶

Find out what is on

la cartelera	entertainments guide	**la guía del ocio**	the guide to what's on

¿Qué se puede hacer el sábado por la tarde?	What is there to do on Saturday evening?
¿Qué ponen en el cine el domingo?	What's on at the cinema on Sunday?
¿Por qué no compras la guía de del ocio?	How about buying the guide to what's on?

Opinions

un descanso	interval	**a causa de**	because of
un éxito	success	**a pesar de**	in spite of
un músico	musician	**francamente**	frankly
el papel	role; part	**no vale la pena**	it's not worth it
una preferencia	choice		

¿Qué te ha parecido el concierto?	What did you think of the concert?
Lo que me gustó más que nada fue la historia.	What I liked above all was the story.
Es una de las mejores películas que he visto.	It's one of the best films I have seen.
El actor que hizo el papel del héroe era fantástico.	The one who played the part of the hero was fantastic.
A pesar de algunos actores muy malos, la obra en sí no era tan mala.	In spite of some bad actors, the play itself wasn't that bad.

Narrate the main features of a film or play

acabar de	to have just	**un ejército**	army
casarse con	to marry	**el futuro**	the future
luchar	to fight; to struggle	**el pasado**	the past
matar	to kill	**un platillo volante**	flying saucer
morir	to die	**un riesgo**	risk
suceder	to happen	**un siglo**	century
un accidente	accident	**antiguamente**	in the past
el amor	love	**por fin**	finally
el día siguiente	the following day	**tan pronto como**	as soon as

Es una película que se desarrolla en el futuro, en el siglo treinta.	It's a film which takes place in the future, in the 30th century.
Al día siguiente el héroe luchó contra el ejército.	The next day, the hero fought the army.
Afortunadamente, no hubo más accidentes.	Fortunately, there were no more accidents.
Tuvo éxito porque se atrevió a tomar riesgos.	She succeeded because she dared to take risks.
Por fin, se casaron.	In the end, they got married.

71

A la prueba

De cine

Lee estos trozos del resumen de las dos películas: (1) Los Picapiedras y (2) Maverick. Decide que trozos corresponden a cada película, y en qué orden aparecen en la versión original.

1.

De cine
'Los Picapiedras'. ¡¡¡Yabba-dabba-dú!!! vuelve la familia más famosa y divertida de la prehistoria. Pedro, Wilma, Pablo, Bam-Bam, Dino y todos los demás

(A) de unos cuantos enemigos que intentan impedírselo. *Maverick* tiene todos los ingredientes que una película del Oeste necesita: indios, pistoleros, caballos y tiroteos en el *saloon* a cuenta de un as que descuidadamente aparece por la manga. Pero no os preocu-

(C) hán abandonado el mundo de los dibujos animados en el que nacieron para convertirse en personajes de carne y hueso. Lo más

(E) Mel Gibson interpreta a un aventurero del viejo oeste que trata de reunir el dinero suficiente para participar en la partida de póquer más importante del país. Por el camino tendrá que librarse

2.

De cine. Maverick. Le habéis visto haciendo de guerrero del futuro en *Mad Max*, o de policía medio loco en la serie *Arma letal*. Ahora el actor Mel Gibson ha cambiado la placa de policía por un caballo y una baraja de cartas. En su última película, *Maverick*,

(B) difícil ha sido trasladar al mundo real los artilugios que utilizaban estos trogloditas. Si el año pasado nos invadió la fiebre prehistórica con *Parque Jurásico*, este verano será de *Los Picapiedra*.

(D) péis, no hay violencia sino mucho sentido del humor ya que todo está contado en un tono de divertida comedia.

Solución en la página 91.

THE WORLD AROUND US

◀ *Home town, local environment and customs* ▶

Understand a description of a town or region

una atracción	attraction	**un palacio**	palace
un bosque	wood; forest	**un reloj**	clock
una capital	capital	**hondo**	deep
una colina	hill	**nacional**	national
el fondo	back; bottom	**profundo**	deep
una frontera	frontier; border	**regional**	regional
una isla	island	**construir**	to build
un lugar de veraneo	summer resort	**faltar**	to lack; to be missing

Your country and others

la agricultura	agriculture	**húmedo**	damp
una biblioteca	library	**orgulloso**	proud
la calidad	quality	**peor**	worse; worst
una cima	summit	**pintoresco**	picturesque
un comercio	shop; business	**seco**	dry
un detalle	detail	**soleado**	sunny
un ferrocarril	railway	**alrededor de**	around
el humo	smoke	**apenas**	hardly
asqueroso	ghastly; awful	**en el centro de**	in the middle of
comercial	commercial	**en todas partes**	everywhere

¿Podrías describir la ciudad que acabas de visitar?	Could you describe the town which you have just visited?
Aquí, en invierno, el clima es seco y soleado.	Here, in winter, the climate is dry and sunny.
El paisaje alrededor del pueblo es muy pintoresco.	The countryside around the town is very picturesque.
¡Es un sitio asqueroso!	It's a ghastly place!

Where you live

un cambio	change	**opinar**	to think about; to have an opinion about
la costa	coast		
limpio	clean		
magnífico	magnificent	**tener vergüenza (de)**	to be ashamed (of)
muerto	dead	**sin embargo**	however
sucio	dirty		

¿Qué opinas de la ciudad donde vives?	What do you think about the town where you live?
Creo que es magnífica porque hay mucho que hacer.	I think it's magnificent because there's lots to do.
A mí me da vergüenza vivir aquí, porque es una ciudad sucia y está muerta.	I'm ashamed to live here because it's a dirty and dead town.
No hay nada que hacer para los jóvenes.	There's nothing for young people to do.

Important festivals

católico	Catholic	la misa del gallo	Midnight Mass
cristiano	Christian	la Noche Vieja	New Year's Eve
judío	Jewish	la sinagoga	synagogue
musulmán	Muslim	disfrazarse	to dress up
protestante	Protestant	recibir	to receive

Vamos a misa.	We go to mass.
Comemos una comida especial.	We eat a special meal.
Nos disfrazamos.	We wear fancy dress.

Weather forecasts

un cambio	change	lluvioso	rainy
un chubasco	downpour	moderado	moderate
el descenso	drop (in temperature)	nuboso	cloudy
el empeoramiento	worsening	superior	above; higher than
la llovizna	drizzle	llover a cántaros	to pour down; to rain cats and dogs
una mejoría	improvement		
la mitad	half	mojarse	to get soaked
la neblina	mist	soplar	to blow
la precipitación	rainfall	volver	to return
un riesgo	risk	el Canal de la Mancha	the English Channel
una tempestad	storm		
una tormenta	storm	el Ebro	the river Ebro
el trueno	thunder	el Estrecho de Gibraltar	the Straits of Gibraltar
la visibilidad	visibility	el Guadalquivir	the river Guadalquivir
borrascoso	stormy		
cubierto	covered; overcast	Lisboa	Lisbon
fresco	cool	el Tajo	the river Tagus
fuerte	'strong; heavy	cielos despejados	clear skies
ligero	slight		

¿Qué dice el pronóstico para mañana?	What does the forecast for tomorrow say?
Parece ser que lloverá.	It seems that it will rain.
Dicen que habrá tormentas y cielos despejados.	They say that there will be storms and clear spells.
Después de mañana, hará buen tiempo y estará soleado.	The day after tomorrow, it will be fine and sunny.
En la mitad sur del país, el cielo estará cubierto.	In the southern half of the country, the sky will be overcast.

A la prueba

El tiempo

Lee este pronóstico del tiempo para España. ¿Qué parte del país tendrá el peor tiempo hoy?

EL SOL			LA LUNA		
Sale	6.51	Barcelona	21.01	Sale	17.08	Barcelona	2.12
	7.16	Madrid	21.24		17.30	Madrid	2.38
	7.29	La Coruña	21.49		17.55	La Coruña	2.51
	8.25	Las Palmas	21.46	Se pone		17.50	Las Palmas	3.50	Se pone

Fase de la Luna — CRECIENTE

Previsión para hoy

Viento del Norte y tormentas en el noreste

El cielo estará nuboso en la cordillera Cantábrica al oeste de los Picos de Europa, y muy nuboso en el este, con intervalos cubiertos y algún chubasco tormentoso; cubierto en Pirineos, con chubascos tormentosos, muy irregulares, durante la tarde, parcialmente nuboso en País Vasco, Cantabria, y con intervalos nubosos en el norte de Navarra, de Aragón y de Cataluña.

Casi despejado en el resto del país. Habrá nieblas matinales en los valles de todas las cordilleras, en el Teide, puntos de la meseta y las zonas costeras. Los vientos serán moderadamente fuertes del Noreste en Canarias. Las temperaturas bajan en Galicia, Cantábrico, Extremadura, Castilla-León, Canarias y algo en centro, sin cambios en el resto. **Europa.** *Londres:* despejado, Noreste flojo, descenso térmico. *Roma:* despejado, nieblas, ascenso térmico. *París:* parcialmente nuboso, descenso térmico. *Francfort:* nubosidad variable.— J. L. RON

El País 6/8/95

Solución en la página 91.

◀ *Finding the way* ▶

How to get to a specific place

una acera	pavement	**un peatón**	pedestrian
un consulado	consulate	**perderse**	to get lost
una lavandería	launderette	**reconocer**	to recognise
una óptica	optician	**sentido único**	one way

¿Exactamente dónde se encuentra el consulado británico?	Where exactly is the British consulate?
Hay que seguir la avenida principal y luego torcer a la derecha a la clínica.	You have to follow the main avenue and then turn right at the clinic.
Será mejor preguntar en la oficina de turismo.	It'll be better to ask at the tourist office.

◀ *Shopping* ▶

Find particular goods and departments within a store

una cartera	wallet	**un escaparate**	shop window
una cazadora	bomber jacket	**un mostrador**	counter
un chaleco	waistcoat	**el papel de escribir**	letter paper; writing paper
el champú	shampoo		
las chanclas	flip-flops	**una perfumería**	perfume shop
la crema de afeitar	shaving cream	**una pila**	battery
un desodorante	deodorant	**la planta**	floor
las escaleras	stairs; escalator	**autoservicio**	self service

¿Dónde está la sección de maquillaje, por favor?	Where is the make-up department, please?
¿Dónde puedo comprar papel de escribir?	Where can I buy some writing paper?
En el sótano.	In the basement.

Discuss shopping habits and preferences

una desventaja	disadvantage		hacer cola	to queue
una ventaja	advantage		mejor	best; better
gustarle más a uno	to like better		peor	worst; worse

El sábado por la tarde, siempre voy al centro comercial.	On Saturday afternoon, I always go to the shopping centre.
En mi opinión, la mejor tienda para ropa es	In my opinion, the best shop for clothes is ... .
En ... las dependientas son más simpáticas.	At ... the shop assistants are nicer.
El supermercado ... queda abierto hasta las veintidós horas.	The ... supermarket stays open until 10 pm.
La desventaja es que esta tienda no abre los domingos.	The disadvantage is that this shop does not open on Sundays.

Return unsatisfactory goods, giving reasons and asking for a refund or replacement

un agujero	hole		reembolsar	to reimburse
una garantía	guarantee		romper	to break
un recibo	receipt		sustituir	to replace
cambiar	to exchange		tener un defecto	to be damaged
devolver el dinero	to give money back		estropeado	spoiled
garantizar	to guarantee		roto	broken; torn

Compré esta cazadora aquí ayer.	I bought this bomber jacket here yesterday.
¿Podría cambiármela?	Could you change it for me?
Mire, está rota.	Look, it's torn.
Sólo vi este agujero cuando llegué a casa.	I only saw this hole when I got home.
¿Me pueden devolver el dinero, por favor?	Can you give me my money back, please?
Me gustaría hablar con el director.	I'd like to talk to the manager.
He guardado el recibo; aquí está.	I've kept the receipt; here it is.

Discounts, special offers, reductions and sales

un descuento	discount		gratuito	free
una oferta especial	special offer		un descuento del diez por ciento	less 10%
una promoción	special price on a new product			
las rebajas	sales			

Las rebajas de enero.	January sales.
Ofertas especiales 'vuelta al cole'.	Special 'back to school' offers.

◀ *Public services* ▶

Sending letters, postcards and parcels

un cartero	postman	**rellenar un**	to fill in a form
un paquete	parcel	**formulario**	
echar (una carta)	to post (a letter)	**Nueva Zelanda**	New Zealand

¿Cuánto costaría enviar este paquete a Nueva Zelanda?	How much would it cost to send this parcel to New Zealand?
¿Quiere enviarlo por avión?	Would you like to send it airmail?

Exchange money or traveller's cheques

un carnet de identidad	identity document	**un dólar**	dollar
		un mostrador	counter
una cuenta bancaria	bank account	**una tarjeta de banco**	bank card
una cuenta corriente	current account	**una tarjeta de crédito**	credit card
una cuenta de ahorros	savings account	**una ventanilla**	window
		aguardar	to expect

¿Cuánto vale la libra esterlina hoy?	How much is the pound sterling worth today?
Quisiera cambiar cien dólares americanos.	I'd like to change 100 American dollars.
¿Qué ventanilla es para cambiar cheques de viaje?	Which window is it to change traveller's cheques.
¿Tiene usted algún documento de identidad?	Do you have any identification document?
Aquí tiene mi pasaporte.	Here's my passport.

Ask for specific currency

un billete de cinco mil pesetas	5,000 peseta note	**una moneda de cien pesetas**	100 peseta coin

¿Podría darme algunas monedas de cincuenta pesetas?	Could you give me some fifty peseta coins?
Me gustaría más tener unos billetes de doscientas pesetas.	I'd prefer some 200 peseta notes.

Report a loss or theft

una cámara de vídeo	video camera	**una recompensa**	reward
una comisaría	police station	**un reloj**	watch
un flash	flash (for a camera)	**un robo**	theft
la forma	shape	**una sortija**	ring
una llave	key	**un talonario de cheques**	cheque book
una maleta	suitcase		
una máquina de fotos	camera	**cuadrado**	square
la marca	make	**de acero inoxidable**	made of stainless steel
una mochila	rucksack		
una oficina de objetos perdidos	lost property office	**de metal**	made of metal
una pulsera	bracelet	**dentro**	inside

en/por todas partes	everywhere		redondo	round
(completamente) nuevo	(brand) new		marcar	to mark
rectangular	rectangular		robar	to steal

He perdido mi cámara de vídeo.	I've lost my video camera.
Me han robado la maleta.	Someone has stolen my case.
Lo perdí antes de ayer.	I lost it the day before yesterday.
La dejé en el autobús.	I left it in the bus.
¿Podría describir su mochila?	Could you describe your rucksack?
Es de color azul claro y bastante grande.	It's light blue and quite big.
¿Qué había dentro?	What was inside it?
Había un talonario de cheques y unas llaves.	There was a cheque book and some keys.
¿De qué marca es la máquina de fotos?	What make is the camera?
La he buscado por todas partes.	I've looked everywhere for it.

◀ *Getting around* ▶

Information about public transport

un coche	carriage (in a train)		un suplemento	supplement
un coche-cama	sleeping car		una tarifa	price; tariff
un coche-restaurante	dining car		un tren de cercanías	slow train stopping at all local stations
un departamento	compartment			
una litera	couchette in a train		a tiempo	on time
un rápido	fast train		perder	to miss
un retraso	delay			

He perdido mi tren.	I've missed my train.
¿A qué hora sale el próximo tren para Granada?	What time does the next train for Granada leave?
¿Hay que pagar un suplemento?	Do you have to pay a supplement?
¿Hay servicio de bar en ese tren?	Is there a buffet service on that train?
Quisiera reservar una litera.	I'd like to reserve a couchette.
¿Es un departamento de no fumadores?	Is it a non-smoking compartment?

Travel by public transport

un auxiliar de vuelo	air steward		el puerto	port; harbour
un hovercraft	hovercraft		un vuelo	flight
un pasajero	passenger		volar	to fly
un piloto	pilot		en clase turista	in tourist class

¿A qué hora sale el próximo barco para Inglaterra?	When does the next boat for England leave?
Quisiera reservar sitio para un coche y tres pasajeros.	I'd like to reserve a place for a car and three passengers.
Quisiera comprar un billete para el próximo vuelo a Londres.	I'd like to buy a ticket for the next flight to London.

Common forms of transport

contaminar	to pollute	un medio de transporte	means of transport
estar mareado	to be seasick	ecológico	ecological
marearse	to get seasick	práctico	handy; practical
tener malestar	to feel sick		

A mí no me gusta coger el barco porque me mareo en seguida.	I don't like taking a boat because I get seasick straight away.
El tren es más ecológico que el autobús.	The train is more ecological than the bus.
Los autobuses contaminan mucho la atmósfera.	Buses badly pollute the atmosphere.
El metro es más rápido y más barato que el autobús.	The underground is faster and cheaper than the bus.

At a service station

el aceite	oil	la mezcla de dos tiempos	two-stroke fuel for motorbikes
el agua	water	una moto	motorbike
el aire	air	un neumático	tyre
una autopista	motorway	la presión	pressure
una batería	car battery	un surtidor	(petrol) pump
un desvío	diversion; detour	conducir	to drive
un escúter	scooter	detener	to stop
una estación de servicio	service station	llenar el depósito	to fill up
el gas-oil	diesel	mirar	to check; to look at
la gasolina	petrol	normal	regular-grade (petrol)
un lavado de coches	automatic car wash	sin plomo	unleaded
un maletero	(car) boot	súper	premium-grade (petrol)
un mapa de carreteras	road map		

Llénelo con gasolina sin plomo.	Fill it up with lead-free.
Dos mil pesetas de súper.	2,000 pesetas worth of premium-grade.
Cuarenta litros de normal.	40 litres of regular-grade petrol.
El surtidor número nueve; ¿qué le debo, por favor?	Pump number nine; how much do I owe you, please?
¿Quiere mirar el agua y el aire?	Would you check the water and the tyre pressures?
¿Para llegar a la autopista, por favor?	How do I get from here to the motorway, please?

A breakdown

un camión	lorry	un motor	motor; engine
una carretera (nacional)	main road	un neumático	tyre
un faro	headlight	el parabrisas	windscreen
un freno	brake	una pieza de recambio	spare part
un limpiaparabrisas	windscreen wiper	un pinchazo	puncture
un mecánico	mechanic	el radiador	radiator

una reparación	repair	señalar	to mark; point out
una rueda	wheel	tardar	to take a long time
una rueda de recambio	spare wheel	tener una avería	to have a mechanical fault
un ruido	noise	averiado	broken down
el volante	steering wheel	extraño	strange
frenar	to brake	pinchado	punctured
funcionar	to work	trasero	back; rear
girar	to turn	algo	something
quedarse sin gasolina	to run out of petrol		

Mi coche está averiado.	My car has broken down.
El motor hace un ruido extraño.	The engine is making a strange noise.
Hay algo que no funciona bien.	Something isn't working properly.
Estamos en la carretera nacional N1, treinta kilómetros al sur de Burgos.	We're on the N1, thirty kilometres south of Burgos.
¿Podría enviar a alguien?	Can you send someone?
¿Cuánto tiempo tardará en arreglarlo?	How long will you take to fix it?

Report an accident

una ambulancia	ambulance	un testigo	witness
un atestado	accident report form	un vehículo	vehicle
los bomberos	fire brigade	una víctima	victim
un carnet de conducir	driving licence	atropellar	to knock down; to run over
un choque	collision	chocar (con)	to bump into; to hit
un cinturón de seguridad	safety belt	circular	to drive
un conductor	driver	patinar	to slip; to skid
el fin	end	reducir la velocidad	to slow down
un herido	injured person	tener miedo	to be afraid; to be frightened
un motociclista	motorcyclist	tener prioridad	to have the right of way
una multa	fine		
las obras	road works	asegurado	insured
un peatón	pedestrian	herido; lesionado	injured
la policía	police	de repente	suddenly
el seguro	insurance	gravemente	seriously
el seguro del coche	car insurance	¡fuego!	fire!
los servicios de urgencia/ emergencia	emergency services	¡socorro!	help!
		vivo	alive

Ha habido un accidente.	There has been an accident.
Es en la autopista A2, diez kilómetros al este de Zaragoza.	It's on motorway A2, ten kilometres east of Zaragoza.
Un camión ha chocado con un coche.	A lorry has hit a car.
El coche estaba parado al lado de la carretera.	The car was stopped at the side of the road.
El camión iba muy rápido.	The lorry was going very fast.
El conductor no pudo parar a tiempo.	The driver couldn't stop in time.
La visibilidad era muy mala.	Visibility was bad.
Hay que llamar a los servicios de urgencia.	We must call for the emergency services.

THE WORLD OF WORK

◀ *Further education and training* ▶

Information about further education and training

un camino	path	**la Selectividad**	(entry exam to higher education)
una cifra	number		
el estado	the state	**un título; una**	degree
los estudios	studies	**licenciatura**	
un ICE	University Institute of Education (for teacher training)	**La UNED**	Spanish equivalent of the Open University
		superior	higher
un IFP	technical college	**universitario**	university (adj.)
un ingeniero	engineer	**alguien**	someone

Discuss education and training

un certificado	certificate	**estar en COU**	to be in the 6th form (Years 12/13)
un diploma	diploma		
los estudios empresariales	business studies	**a gusto**	happy; at ease
una facultad (de medicina)	(medical) faculty		

¿Has estado a gusto en el colegio?	Have you been happy at school?
Sí, gran parte del tiempo ha estado bien.	Yes, most of the time it's been fine.
Sobre todo me han gustado las ciencias.	I've especially liked the sciences.
¿Qué piensas hacer el año que viene?	What are you thinking of doing next year?
Espero estudiar el COU.	I hope to prepare for my A-levels.
Si me aprueban en los exámenes, iré a la universidad.	If I pass my exams, I'll go to university.
¿Qué piensas estudiar en la universidad?	What are you thinking of studying at university?
No lo sé todavía: medicina o química quizás.	I don't know yet: medicine or chemistry, perhaps.

◀ *Careers and employment* ▶

Explain choice of study or training

una duda	doubt	**capaz**	capable
un laboratorio (de idiomas)	(language) laboratory	**flojo**	weak
		fuerte	good at; strong
una nota	mark	**probar**	to prove
el progreso	progress	**(casi) seguro**	(almost) certainly

¿Qué vas a hacer el año que viene?	What are you going to do next year?
¿Qué asignaturas vas a estudiar?	Which subjects are you going to study?
Si todo va bien en los exámenes, casi seguro que estudiaré historia, español y económicas.	If I do well in my exams, I'll almost certainly study history, Spanish and economics.
Siempre saco buenas notas en matemáticas.	I always get good marks in maths.

Express hopes and plans for the future

la enseñanza	teaching	creer	to believe
un futuro	future	ganarse la vida	to earn one's living
una manera	way	obligatorio	compulsory

¿Qué esperas hacer más tarde?	What do you hope to do later?
No veo mi futuro muy claro.	I don't see my future very clearly.
En los próximos meses voy a trabajar mucho para mis exámenes.	In the coming months I'm going to work hard for my exams.
Al terminar mis estudios obligatorios, me gustaría ir a la universidad.	At the end of my compulsory schooling, I'd like to go to university.
Me gustaría sacar un trabajo para ganarme la vida.	I'd like to get a job and earn my living.

Jobs and work experience

una entrevista	interview	gastar	to spend
la formación	training	a tiempo parcial	part-time
un puesto	job; post	de medio tiempo	half-time
un taller	workshop	de tiempo completo	full-time
(ser) cansado	(to be) tiring		

¿Por qué trabaja usted el fin de semana?	Why do you work at the weekend?
Trabajo porque me gusta tener dinero para gastar.	I work because I like to have money to spend.
Ya he trabajado en una cafetería.	I've already worked in a café.
El trabajo es interesante pero cansado.	The work is interesting but tiring.
Busco un trabajo a tiempo parcial.	I'm looking for a part-time job.

Opinions about different jobs

una ambición	ambition	un(a) peluquero/a	hairdresser
el comercio	commerce	un pintor	decorator
un(a) empleado/a	employee	la seguridad	security
una granja	farm	un sindicato	trade union
los negocios	business	llegar a ser	to become

Ser mecanógrafa es un buen empleo.	Being a typist is a very good job.
La vida de un obrero es dura.	A workman's life is hard.
Parece que los peluqueros ganan un buen sueldo.	It appears that hairdressers earn a good wage.
Para mí, la seguridad es esencial.	For me, security is essential.

Enquire about the availability of suitable work

un curriculum	CV	libre	vacant
un salario	salary	permanente	permanent
una situación	situation	temporal	temporary

¿Tendría usted un puesto libre?	Would you have a vacancy?
Haré lo que sea.	I'll do anything.
Estaré libre a partir del primero de agosto.	I'll be free from the 1st of August.
¿Podría darme algunos detalles del salario?	Could you give me some details about the salary?
Tengo experiencia de trabajo en unos almacenes en Inglaterra.	I've already worked in department stores in England.
Busco un trabajo temporal.	I'm looking for a temporary job.

Occupations

una acomodadora	cinema usherette	un(a) frutero/a	fruit seller
un agricultor	agricultural worker	un militar	soldier
un bombero	fire fighter		

¿En qué trabaja tu madre?	What does your mother do for a living?
Trabaja en una biblioteca.	She works in a library.
Mi padrastro es militar: está en las fuerzas aéreas.	My stepfather is a soldier: he's in the air force.
Mi hermano antes era bombero.	My brother used to be a fire fighter.

Advantages and disadvantages

una desventaja	disadvantage	bien (mal) pagado	well (badly) paid
una ventaja	advantage	seguro	secure

A menudo las enfermeras tienen que trabajar de noche.	Nurses often have to work at night.
La enseñanza es un empleo bastante seguro y bien pagado.	Teaching is quite secure and well paid.
La jornada de un agricultor puede ser muy larga.	A farm worker's day can be very long.
La ventaja es que los médicos están bien pagados.	The advantage is that doctors are well paid.
Si yo tuviera que trabajar en una fábrica, no estaría muy contento.	If I had to work in a factory, I wouldn't be very happy.

◀ *Advertising and publicity* ▶

Advertisements

un anuncio	TV commercial	exigir	to require; to demand
un contable	accountant		
la venta	sale; selling	guardar	to keep

A la prueba

According to this advertisement, what do AVE-RENFE promise to do?

Solución en la página 91.

Le Devolvemos el
IMPORTE TOTAL
De SU Billete
Si llegamos con <u>más</u> de
5 MIN.
de RETRASO*

Aunque dudamos mucho que se vaya a llevar esta alegría. Porque siempre hemos apostado por la puntualidad. Por no hacerle perder ni un minuto de su tiempo. Por eso, AVE se compromete a devolverle el importe total de su billete si el tren tiene un retraso superior a 5 minutos. Una razón más para seguir siendo puntuales. Por la cuenta que nos trae. **AVE**
SUBE MAS ALTO

Anuario El País 1995 p.227

◄ *Communication* ►

Using the phone, fax or E-mail

el correo electrónico	E-mail	**descolgar el**	to pick up the
un modem	modem	**teléfono**	receiver
un ordenador	computer	**llamar**	to call
un segundo	second	**marcar el número**	to dial the number
un telefax	fax machine	**ponerse en**	to get in touch (with)
el tono de marcar	dialling tone	**contacto (con)**	
colgar	to replace the receiver	**no cuelgue(s)**	hold the line; don't hang up

Siempre puede ponerse en contacto conmigo por teléfono.	You can always contact me by telephone.
Envíeme un mensaje por correo electrónico.	Send me a message by E-mail.
¿Cuál es su número de fax?	What's your fax number?
Encontrará nuestro número en la guía telefónica.	You'll find our number in the directory.
Llámeme mañana si usted está libre.	Call me tomorrow if you're free.

Obtain coins or a phone-card

una cabina telefónica	phone booth	**una tarjeta para el teléfono**	phone-card
una moneda de cien pesetas	100 peseta coin	**una unidad**	unit

¿Podría dejarme unas monedas de cien pesetas para el teléfono?	Could you let me have some 100 peseta coins for the phone?
Una tarjeta para el teléfono, por favor.	A phone-card, please.

THE INTERNATIONAL WORLD

◀ *Life in other countries and communities* ▶

Typical foods

la charcutería	pork meats	**la pastelería**	pastries
la harina	flour	**una receta**	recipe
un horno	oven	**cocinar**	to cook
un ingrediente	ingredient	**mezclar**	to mix
un melón	melon	**picante**	spicy
una merienda	picnic	**suave**	mild
(campestre)		**variado**	varied

Un plato típico de mi país es Yorkshire pudding.	A typical dish from my country is Yorkshire pudding.
Es un tipo de crêpe.	It's a sort of pancake.
Se come con ternera como plato principal, o con mermelada como postre.	It's eaten with beef as a main course, or with jam as a dessert.
Se hace con harina, agua, huevos y sal.	You make it with flour, water, eggs and salt.
Hay que mezclar los ingredientes con un tenedor.	You have to mix the ingredients with a fork.
Y luego se cocina en un horno muy caliente.	And then it's cooked in a very hot oven.

Important social conventions

una costumbre	custom	**¡a la tuya!**	to your good health! (informal)
dar el pésame	to offer condolences		
¡salud!	good health!	**¡a la suya!**	to your good health! (formal)

¿Cuándo uno come en España, hay alguna costumbre particular?	When eating in Spain, are there any special conventions?
Ponemos el pan en la mesa. Normalmente no hay ningún plato especial.	We put bread on the table. Normally there isn't a special plate.

◀ *Tourism* ▶

Information about excursions

informarse	to get information	**recoger**	to pick up
ir de excursión	to go for a trip	**con guía**	guided

Quisiéramos visitar los Pirineos.	We'd like to visit the Pyrenees region.
Hay una excursión con guía para pasado mañana.	There's a guided excursion for the day after tomorrow.
¿El precio del alojamiento está incluido?	Is the price of accommodation included?

Request tourist publicity

un camping	campsite	**un sitio de interés**	beauty spot; a site of historical or archaeological interest
una estrella	one star		
un mapa	map		
tener la intención	to intend		

Muy señor mío:
Tengo la intención de pasar unos días en su región con mi familia, en el mes de julio.
¿Podría enviarme información sobre los campings de la zona, unos folletos sobre los
sitios de interés que se pueden visitar, y detalles de las excursiones que se pueden realizar en la
zona?
Le saluda atentamente:

¿Tiene un mapa de la región?	Do you have a map of the region?
¿Qué hay de interés en la zona?	What is there of interest in the area?
¿Tiene unos folletos sobre la ciudad?	Do you have any leaflets about the town?

Opinions about excursions and places of interest

un cuadro	painting	**alrededor**	around
el interés	interest	**preferido**	favourite
un lugar de veraneo	summer holiday destination		

¿Qué hay que ver en la región?	What is there to see in the region?
Mi lugar de veraneo preferido es	My favourite summer holiday destination is ....
El museo tiene una buena colección de cuadros del siglo diecinueve.	The museum has a a good collection of nineteenth-century paintings.
El paisaje alrededor es muy pintoresco.	The surrounding countryside is very picturesque.

Discuss a holiday: past or future

un insecto	insect	**volver**	to return
una mosca	fly	**mucha gente**	a lot of people
el polvo	dust	**al extranjero**	abroad
un propietario	owner	**desilusionado**	disappointed

Fuimos a África del Norte.	We went to North Africa.
Fue un desastre debido al calor y a los insectos.	It was a disaster due to the heat and the insects.
Nos quedamos bastante desilusionados.	We were quite disappointed.
¿Adónde irán ustedes el año que viene?	Where will you go next year?
Seguramente iremos al extranjero.	We'll no doubt go abroad.

Express preferences for different holidays

activo	active		**elegir**	to choose
amueblado	furnished		**estar harto de**	to be sick of
lujoso	luxurious; luxury		**es mejor**	it's better

Yo prefiero ir de vacaciones al extranjero.	I prefer to go abroad on holiday.
En mi opinión, es mejor quedarse en Gran Bretaña.	In my opinion, it's better to stay in Britain.
Me encantaría ir a un hotel muy lujoso.	I'd love to go to a very luxurious hotel.
Me gustaría más alquilar un apartamento amueblado.	I'd rather rent a furnished flat.
No me gustan nada las vacaciones activas.	I hate active holidays.
Si pudiera elegir, iría siempre a España.	If I had the choice, I'd always go to Spain.
Estoy harto de quedarme en casa.	I'm sick of staying at home.

◀ *Accommodation* ▶

Arrange accommodation at hotels, youth hostels and campsites

los cubos de basura	rubbish bins		**una tienda de camping**	tent
un enchufe	electric plug		**acampar**	to camp
un hornillo de gas (butano)	camping gas cooker		**a la sombra**	in the shade
una mochila	rucksack		**bien equipado**	well equipped
un parque infantil	children's playground		**municipal**	municipal
una sábana	sheet		**vigilado**	supervised
un saco de dormir	sleeping bag		**por día**	per day
un sitio	site; location; plot		**por persona**	per person

¿Tiene sitio para dos adultos y un niño?	Do you have room for two adults and one child?
Lo siento, pero está completo.	I'm sorry, but it's full.
Necesitamos un sitio grande para nuestra tienda de camping.	We need a big site for our tent.
Se puede alquilar sábanas y un saco de dormir.	You can hire sheets and a sleeping bag.
¿Cuánto es por persona por día?	How much is it per person per day?
Todavía hay sitio en el camping municipal.	There is still room at the municipal campsite.

Rules and regulations

un bloque sanitario	toilet block	una sala de juegos	games room
una cocina de gas	gas cooker	una salida de	emergency exit
un colchón de aire	inflatable mattress; air bed	emergencia	
el encargado	warden	atar	to tie (up)
el humo	smoke	fumar	to smoke
un incendio	fire	molestar	to disturb; to inconvenience
un lavabo	wash basin	para llevarse	to take away
un máquina de afeitar	electric razor	ponerse en contacto con	to contact
una pila	washing-up sink	en caso de	in case of
un reglamento	rule	potable	drinking; drinkable

En caso de incendio, salga en seguida por la salida de emergencia más cercana.	In the event of fire, leave at once through the nearest emergency exit.
No use el ascensor.	Do not use the lift.
El último día, hay que desalojar la habitación antes de mediodía.	On the last day, you have to leave the room before midday.
Todo el mundo debe ayudar con la faena.	Everyone must help with the housework.
No debe haber ningún ruido a partir de las diez de la noche.	There must be no noise after 10 pm.
Prohibido fumar en los dormitorios.	Smoking is forbidden in the dormitories.
Esta agua no es potable.	This water is not drinkable.
En caso de problema, ponerse en contacto con el encargado.	If there are any problems, contact the warden.
Deje limpios los lavabos.	Leave the wash basins clean.

◄ *The wider world* ►

Environmental issues

una ballena	whale	la protección	protection
una bomba	bomb	una prueba	test
una central eléctrica	power station	un tigre	tiger
un delfín	dolphin	un zoo	zoo
un elefante	elephant	dar miedo	to frighten
una encuesta	survey	proteger	to protect
un león	lion	reciclar	to recycle
el medio ambiente	environment	apasionado por	really concerned about
la naturaleza	nature	en peligro	in danger; endangered
un océano	ocean	interesado en	interested in
un(a) panda	panda	nuclear	nuclear
un planeta	planet		
una presentación	presentation		

A la prueba

Encuentras este artículo en una revista española. Explica a un amigo que no habla español el significado de la campaña Bandera Azul.

Campaña Bandera Azul de España

La campaña Bandera Azul de Europa es desarrollada desde el Año Europeo del Medio Ambiente (1987) por la Fundación Europea de Educación Ambiental (FEEE), en España ADEAC-FEEE, con el patrocinio y apoyo técnico de la Comisión Europea.

JOSÉ R. SÁNCHEZ MORO

La concesión de la Bandera Azul da derecho a enarbolarla durante un año a aquellas playas y puertos limpios y seguros, que demuestran su preocupación por una gestión y educación ambiental, y cuya candidatura es aprobada por un jurado nacional y, posteriormente, por el jurado internacional. En 1993, de entre unas 450 candidaturas españolas, han obtenido la Bandera Azul 229 playas y 51 puertos deportivos.

Los criterios de concesión, resumidos en 12 pictogramas, se agrupan en cuatro categorías:

– Excelente calidad de aguas de baño.

– Servicios relacionados con la seguridad: limpieza, salvamento y socorrismo, señalización, ausencia de animales domésticos y de cámping salvaje, etcétera.

– Información y educación ambiental.

– Cumplimiento de la legislación litoral: Ley de Costas, Espacios y Especies Protegidas, reglamentación autonómica y local.

Playas españolas con Bandera Azul

POR AÑOS	Número	% Incremento
1988	106	63,08
1989	120	13,21
1990	148	23,33
1991	170	14,86
1992	206	21,18
1993	229	11,17

POR CC.AA/Provincias 1993	Número	% Incremento
CATALUÑA	9	3,93
Gerona	1	0,44
Barcelona	3	1,31
Tarragona	5	2,18
BALEARES	55	24,02
Mallorca	30	13,10
Ibiza	10	4,37
Menorca	10	4,37
Formentera	5	2,18
C.VALENCIANA	59	25,76
Castellón	9	3,93
Valencia	15	6,55
Alicante	35	15,28

POR CC.AA/Provincias 1993	Número	% Incremento
MURCIA	10	4,37
ANDALUCÍA	39	17,03
Almería	14	6,11
Granada	2	0,87
Málaga	12	5,24
Cádiz	7	3,06
Huelva	4	1,75
CANARIAS	7	3,06
Tenerife	3	1,31
Gran Canaria	4	1,75
GALICIA	31	13,54
Pontevedra	7	3,06
La Coruña	14	6,11
Lugo	10	4,37
ASTURIAS	2	0,87
CANTABRIA	13	5,68
PAÍS VASCO	4	1,75
Vizcaya	2	0,87
Guipúzcoa	2	0,87
Total	**229**	**100,00**

Fuente: Fundación para la Educación y Medio Ambiente en Europa.

Anuario El País 1993

Solución en la página 91.

Understand global issues

la ayuda	aid; help	el plomo	lead
el azufre	sulphur	el presidente	president
el carbón	coal	el primer ministro	prime minister
la contaminación	pollution	el racismo	racism
un contaminante	pollutant	un(a) refugiado/a	refugee
el crimen	crime	la religión	religion
una crisis	crisis	el SIDA	Aids
la culpa	fault; blame	la supervisión	supervision
el daño	damage	el terrorismo	terrorism
las drogas	drugs	la tolerancia	tolerance
la economía	the economy	la violencia	violence
una elección	election	declarar	to declare
el gamberrismo	hooliganism	denunciar	to report
los gases de escape	exhaust fumes	en cuanto a	as for
un nivel	level	interesado por	concerned about
la ONU	UNO	internacional	international
una organización	organisation	reciente	recent
la paz	peace		

Estoy apasionado por el medio ambiente. — I'm really concerned about the environment.

Es imprescindible proteger los animales en peligro. — It is essential to protect endangered animals.

Todo el mundo debe luchar contra la contaminación de nuestro planeta. — Everyone should fight against the pollution of our planet.

En casa, reciclamos todas las botellas y los periódicos. — At home, we recycle all the bottles and newspapers.

Las centrales nucleares me dan miedo. — Nuclear power stations frighten me.

Discuss any part of Spain you know about

el gobierno	government	inaceptable	unacceptable
un habitante	inhabitant	en medio de	in the middle of
un impuesto	tax	me es igual	it's all the same to me; I don't care
considerar	to consider; to think		
construir	to build	no vale la pena	it's not worth it; there's no point
protestar	to protest		
extraordinario	amazing	sin embargo	however

Es una ciudad situada en el norte de España. — It's a town situated in the north of Spain.

El gobierno quiere construir una autopista alrededor de la ciudad. — The government wants to build a motorway round the town.

Dentro de poco habrá una central nuclear allí. — There will soon be a nuclear power station there.

Los habitantes lo consideran inaceptable. — The inhabitants find that unacceptable.

En mi opinión, no vale la pena protestar. — In my opinion, it's not worth protesting.

A la prueba

Reglas de oro para cuidar el medio ambiente.
Empareja cada consejo con el dibujo más apropiado.

1

Deposita los periódicos viejos y las botellas de vidrio en los contenedores públicos. Ya en casi todas las ciudades hay recogida de papel y vidrio. Tú mismo puedes llevar a los contenedores de la calle lo que vayas recogiendo en casa.

2

Usar transporte público ayuda al medio ambiente. La contaminación del aire disminuye si usamos menos los vehículos particulares. Si utilizas autobuses, metro y tranvías pondrás tu granito de arena para que mejore la calidad del aire.

3

Si apagas la luz cuando no la necesites, la atmósfera te lo agradecerá. La energía eléctrica se produce en centrales térmicas, que contaminan la atmósfera, o nucleares, que son peligrosas. Ahorrar, incluso el gasto de una bombilla, es importante.

4

. No dejes en el bosque la huella de tu paso. Resulta agradable acampar, comer y pasear por el bosque. Pero recuerda que todo lo que lleves al campo debe volver contigo, especialmente las bolsas y los envases.

5

Lleva tu propia bolsa y rechaza las de plástico. Cada español usa más de 200 bolsas de plástico al año, que luego terminan abandonadas en cualquier sitio. Acostúmbrate a usar tus propios envases y contenedores.

6

Evita hacer ruidos innecesarios. La contaminación acústica resulta una de las más amplias, molestas y difíciles de corregir. No añadas ruido en tu tiempo de ocio, ni con tu bicicleta, ni con tu moto, ni en los locales públicos.

A
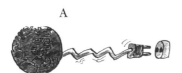

B

C

D

E

F

Pequeño País No 658; 660; 662; 663

Solución en la página 91.

◀ *Solutions* ▶

Para mejorar la memoria 1
Página 4

Hay dieciocho bolígrafos
Tu respuesta:
La respuesta correcta en menos de 30 segundos:
¡Sobresaliente!
La respuesta correcta en menos de 40 segundos:
¡Bien!
La respuesta correcta en más de cuarenta segundos:
¡No te desanimes! La próxima vez intenta concentrarte más y trabajar con calma.

Para mejorar la memoria 2
Página 8

Hay quince bicicletas.
Tu respuesta:
La respuesta correcta en menos de 30 segundos:
¡Muy bien!
La respuesta correcta en 30 segundos:
¡Bien!
La respuesta correcta en más de 30 segundos: Continúa con los ejercicios. También podrías inventar otros ejercicios para hacer; por ejemplo:
• para mejorar la memoria auditiva, escucha la radio e intenta decir quién habla (también puedes hacer este ejercicio con el teléfono).
• para mejorar la memoria visual, cierra los ojos e intenta ver una calle por donde pasas cada día. ¿Qué edificios ves? O piensa en tu dormitorio, ¿puedes describirlo en detalle?

Para mejorar la memoria 3
Página 15

1 una película policíaca
2 el desayuno
3 Inglaterra
4 el Reino Unido
5 el dormitorio
6 un cepillo de dientes
7 un lavaplatos
8 una butaca
9 emocionante
10 la natación

Respuestas correctas:
8 a 10: ¡Muy bien!
5 a 7: ¡Bien!
0 a 4: hay que mejorar más tu memoria verbal. ¿Qué se puede hacer?
Es fácil. Un compañero, o tu profesor puede preparar otra actividad parecida a ésta, basándola en las palabras que hay en este libro.
Luego, repite el mismo ejercicio con la lista nueva.

Para mejorar la memoria 4
Página 26

Las tres letras son-*ion*, y las palabras son distrac*ción*, vaca*ciones*, reg*ión*, e informa*ción*.

Para mejorar la memoria 5
Página 30

1 un perro
2 una bicicleta
3 un piano
4 una piscina
5 una playa
6 unas gafas de sol
8 la aduana
9 una plaza de toros
10 un monopatín

¿Estás contento con el resultado? Si no, piensa en lo que puedes hacer para mejorarlo.

Para mejorar la memoria 6
Página 35

A2: Hace sol; está despejado.
B3: Llueve; está lloviendo.
C1: Hace viento.
B1: Hay tormenta

Para mejorar la memoria 7
Página 47

Un autobús, una oficina, una tienda, un periódico, una enfermera, una mecanógrafa, una camarera, un torero, un mecánico, una guía telefónica, un folleto, un partido (de fútbol)
Respuestas correctas:
10–12: ¡Muy bien!
5–9: ¡Bien!
0–4: ¡Ay!

A la prueba

página 18: 275 pesetas

página 38: C) ¿Cuánto es en total, por favor?

página 40: B) Llama a cobro revertido.

página 42: The 'Tren Azul' leaves every 30 minutes.

página 45: B) En autocar.

página 52: Fui a la playa (a la costa) con mi familia.

página 59: *Billy y el vestido rosa* is about a young boy whose mother one day sends him to school wearing a pink dress. At school nobody seems to notice except Billy. What happens during the day makes Billy realise some of the advantages and disadvantages of being a girl.

página 60: 1 A las 21.30.
2 En Canal +.
3 Cuéntame cómo pasó.

página 71: 1CB; 2EAD.

página 74: En el noreste – en los Pirineos.

página 83: AVE-RENFE promises to reimburse the cost of your ticket if the high speed train arrives more than 5 minutes late, provided that the delay is their fault.

página 88: The 'Bandera Azul' (Blue Flag) is awarded each year to the cleanest beaches, ports and harbours in Spain.

página 90: 1C; 2E; 3A; 4F; 5D; 6B.